Paris Ontario Book 3 in Colour Photos, Saving Our History One Photo at a Time

Photography
by Barbara Raué
2017

Series Name:
Cruising Ontario

Book 25: Paris Book 3, Harrisburg and Glen Morris

Cover photo: 87 Willow Street, Page 13

Series Name: Cruising Ontario
Saving Our History One Photo at a Time
in colour photos

Books Available in Alphabetical Order:
Aberfoyle, Acton, Alton, Amherstburg, Ancaster, Arthur, Aylmer, Ayr, Bloomingdale, Brantford, Burlington, Caledon, Caledonia, Cambridge, Clifford, Conestogo, Delhi, Dorchester to Aylmer, Drayton, Drumbo, Dryden, Dundas, Eden Mills, Elmira, Elora, Essex, Fergus, Guelph, Hagersville, Hamilton, Hanover, Harriston, Hespeler, Jarvis, Kenora, Kingston, Kingsville, Kitchener, Linwood, Listowel, London, Lucknow, Midland, Mono, Mount Forest, Neustadt, New Hamburg, Niagara-on-the-Lake, Oakville, Orangeville, Orillia, Ottawa, Owen Sound, Palmerston, Penetanguishene, Peterborough, Petrolia, Port Elgin, Preston, Rockwood, Sarnia, Seaforth, Sheffield, Shelburne, Simcoe, Southampton, St. Jacobs, St. Marys, St. Thomas, Stoney Creek, Stratford, Thamesford, Tillsonburg, Waterdown, Waterford, Waterloo, Welland, Wellesley, Windsor, Wingham, Woodstock

Book 157: Brockville
Book 158: Merrickville
Book 159: Smiths Falls
Book 160: Portland, Newboro
Book 161: Westport & Area
Book 162: Perth
Book 163-166: Belleville
Book 167-168: Port Colborne
Book 169: Erin in Colour
Book 170: Goderich in Colour
Book 171: Sault Ste. Marie
Book 172: Lake Superior
Book 173-176: Thunder Bay

Book 177-179: Paris

Other Books by Barbara Raue

Coins of Gold

Arrows, Indians and Love

The Life and Times of Barbara
Volume 1: Inventions That Have Enhanced My Life
Volume 2: Entertainment That I Have Enjoyed
Volume 3: East Coast Trips
Volume 4: Olympics Have Always Intrigued Me
Volume 5: Wonders of the World
Volume 6: Caribbean Cruises We Have Enjoyed
Volume 7: Animals
Volume 8: Storms and Other Major Disasters in My Lifetime
Volume 9: Wars, Terrorist Attacks and Major Disasters

The Cromwell Family Book

Laura Secord Discovered

Daddy Where Are You?

Montana Series
Book 1: Montana Dream
Book 2: Life on the Montana Frontier
Book 3: Montana to Boston and Back
Book 4: Montana Sons Go to War
Book 5: Montana Sons Return From War

Visit Barbara's website to view all of her books
http://barbararaue.ca

Paris

Paris, Ontario is located on the Grand River. It was first settled by Hiram Capron a native of Vermont who, in 1822, emigrated to Norfolk County where he helped to establish one of Upper Canada's earliest iron foundries. He settled here at the Forks of the Grand (where the Grand and Nith Rivers meet) in 1829, divided part of his land into town lots, and in 1830 constructed a grist-mill and named the town after the gypsum deposits that were mined nearby. Gypsum is used to make plaster of Paris.

Records from 1846 indicate that the settlement, in a hilly area called Oak Plains, was divided into the upper town and the lower town. In addition to successful farmers in the area, the community of 1,000 people (Americans, Scottish, English, and Irish) was thriving. Manufacturing had already begun, with industries powered by the river. A great deal of plaster was being exported and there were three mills, a tannery, a woolen factory, a foundry, and many tradesmen. Five churches had been built; and the post office was receiving mail three times a week.

While the telephone was invented at Brantford, Ontario in 1874, Alexander Graham Bell made the first transmission to a distance between Brantford and Paris on August 3, 1876.

The use of cobblestones to construct buildings was introduced to the area by Levi Boughton when he erected St. James Church in 1839; this was the first cobblestone structure in Paris. Two churches and ten homes, all in current use, are made of numerous such stones taken from the rivers. Other architectural styles that are visible in the downtown area include Edwardian, Gothic and Post Modern.

The Township of South Dumfries is situated in the north part of the County of Brant. The earliest settlements were in and around the Village of St. George. Two vital factors of the area which caused settlers to locate here were flowing wells and excellent farm land.

The first establishments in the township were a grist mill in 1817, a distillery in 1818, a grocery store in 1820, a log school in 1823, and a post office in 1833. The first church was opened as a Baptist Church in 1824. The Village of Harrisburg was laid out in 1855 at the junction of the Wellington, Grey & Bruce and Great Western railways. Glen Morris was laid out in 1848 on the banks of the Grand River twelve miles from Brantford.

Harrisburg

In the mid-1800s, Harrisburg was a stop on the Great Western Railway serving as a shipping point for St. George and area. About 1854, a branch line twelve miles long from Harrisburg to Galt opened and Harrisburg got its first train station. In 1882, the Great Western Railway was absorbed by the Grand Trunk Railway.

Glen Morris

The village of Glen Morris is on both sides of the Grand River with most of the historical buildings on the east side along East River Road. Glen Morris was first known as Dawson's Bridge as it was John Dawson who built a sawmill and bridge in 1833 across the Grand River. In 1840, the settlement was renamed Middleton. Samuel Latshaw laid out the village in 1848 and in 1851 it was named Glen Morris in honor of their Postmaster.

Table of Contents

Paris, Ontario
    Baird Street — Page 7
    Willow Street — Page 10
    St. Andrew Street — Page 14
    Homestead Road — Page 24
    Oak Avenue — Page 25
    Keg Lane Road — Page 26
    West River Road — Page 27
    Kitchen School Road — Page 29

Harrisburg — Page 30
    Harrisburg Road
    German School Road

Glen Morris — Page 34
    McPherson School Road
    Dunbar Street
    East River Road
    Princess Street
    West Dumfries Road
    Pinehurst Road
    Paris Plains Church Road
    Watts Pond Road

Architectural Terms — Page 48

Building Styles — Page 52

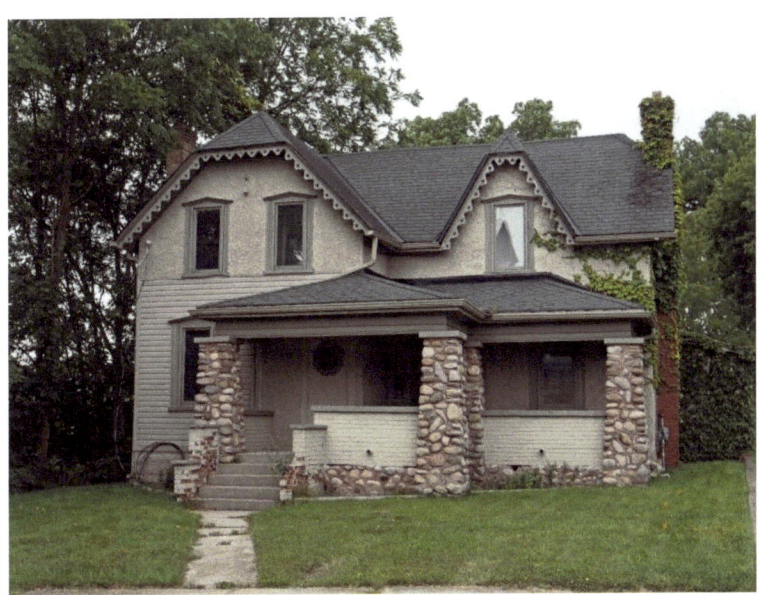

Baird Street – Gothic style with verge board trim on chipped gables, cobblestone pillars supporting verandah

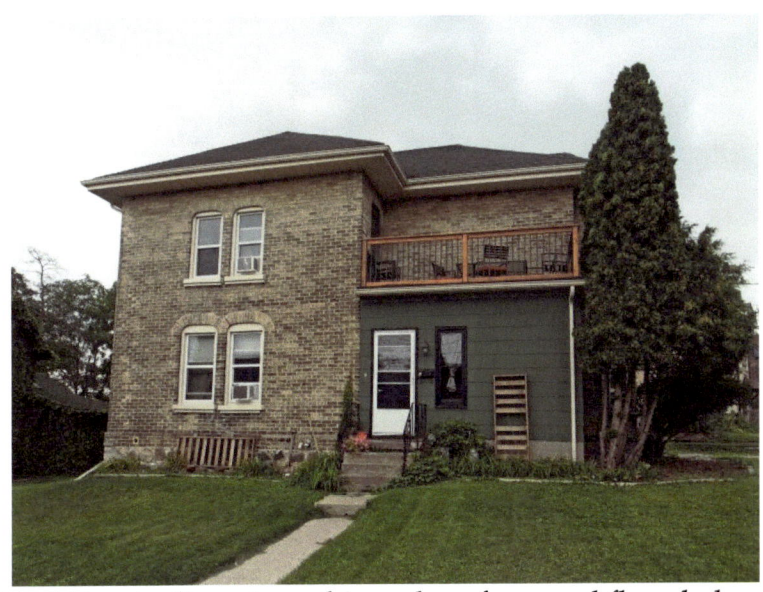

Baird Street – limestone, hipped roof, second floor balcony

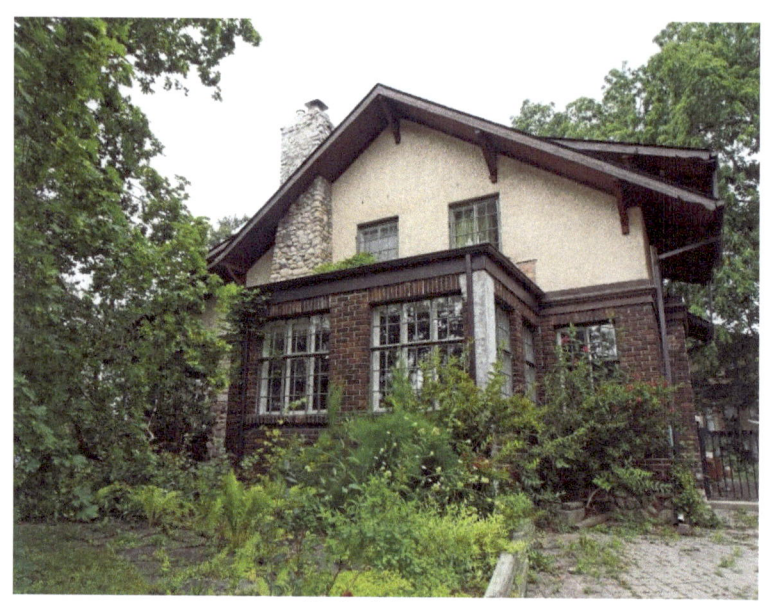

Baird Street

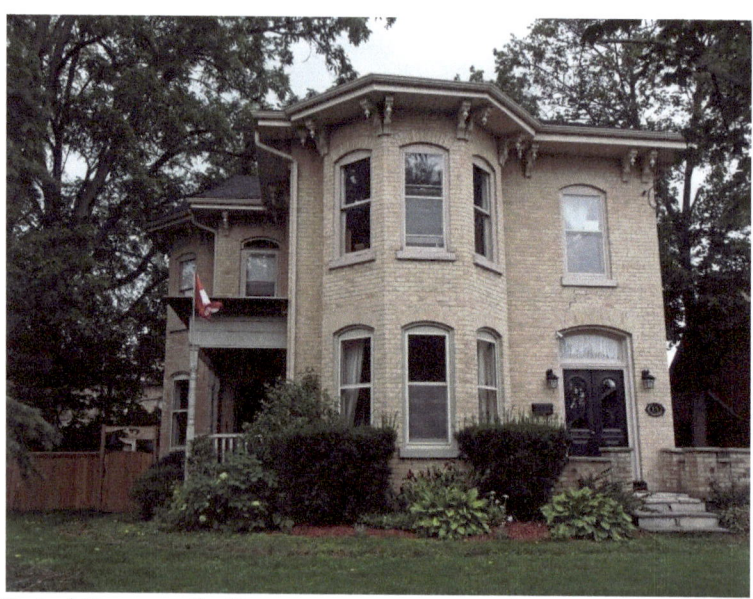

15 Baird Street – Italianate – two-storey bay window, cornice brackets

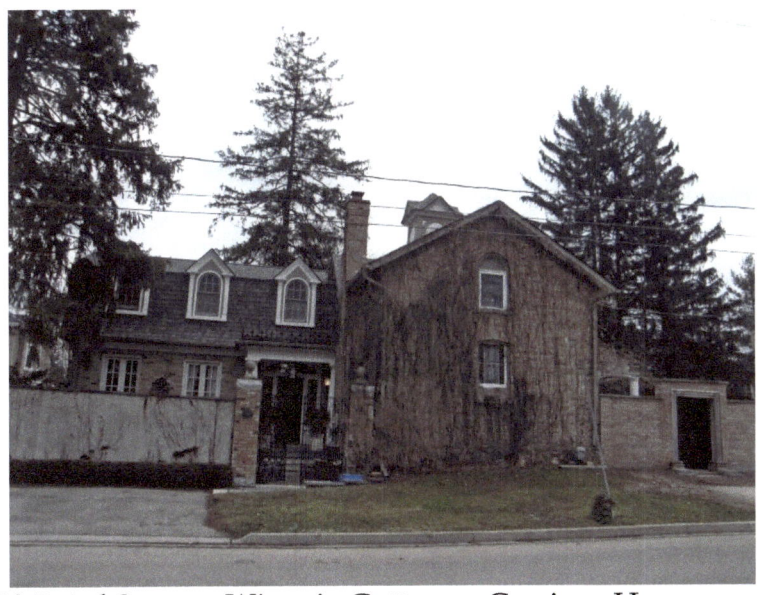

18 Baird Street – Wisteria Cottage – Carriage House now separate from 194 Grand River Street North (behind)

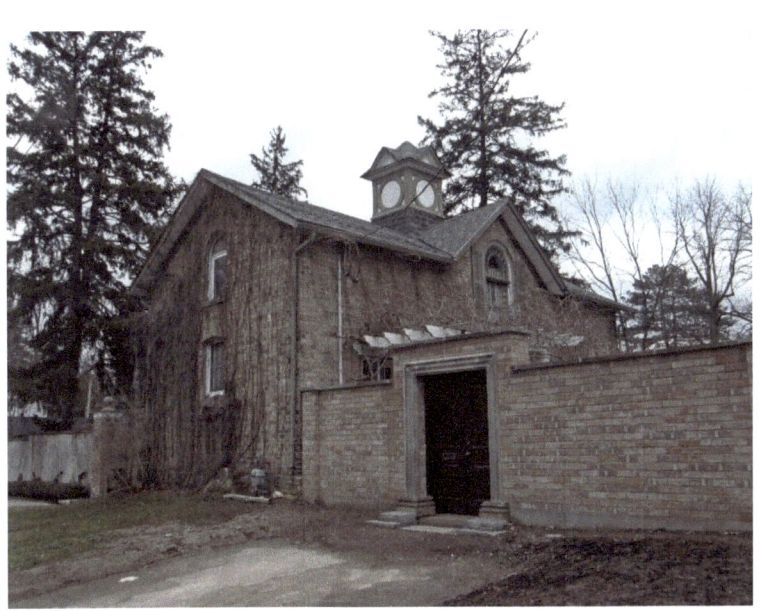

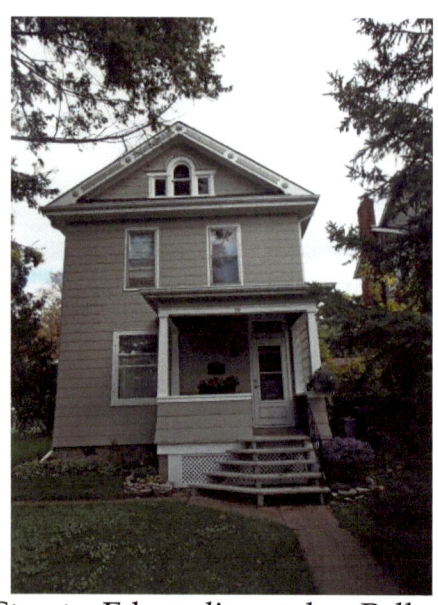

111 Willow Street – Edwardian style – Palladian window

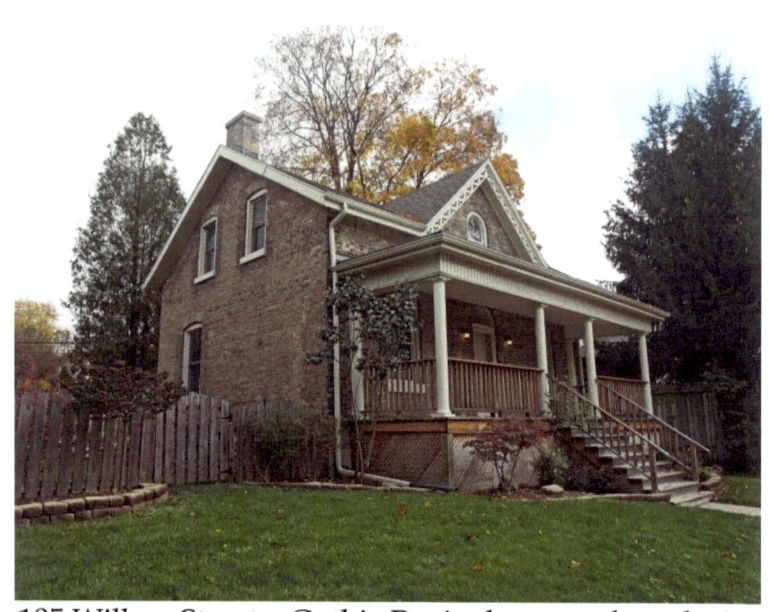

105 Willow Street – Gothic Revival – verge board trim

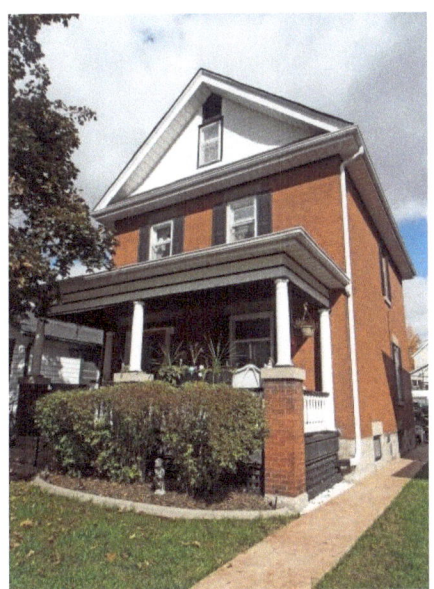

95 Willow Street - Edwardian

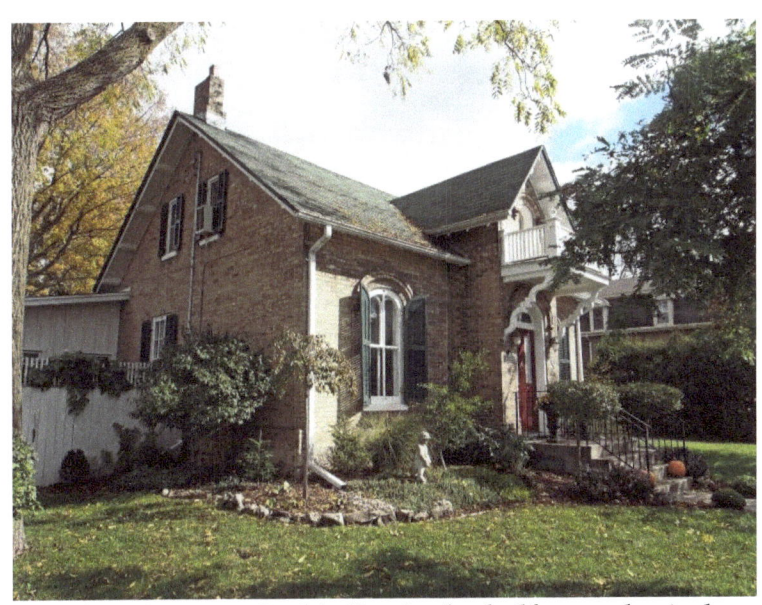

89 Willow Street – Gothic Revival – half-round windows, yellow brick

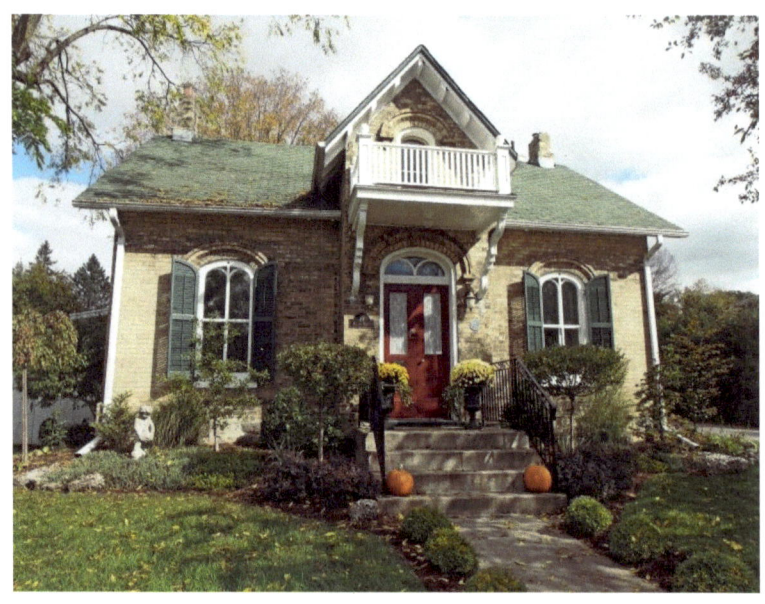

89 Willow Street - Gothic Revival, 1½ storey, half-round windows, transom window above door

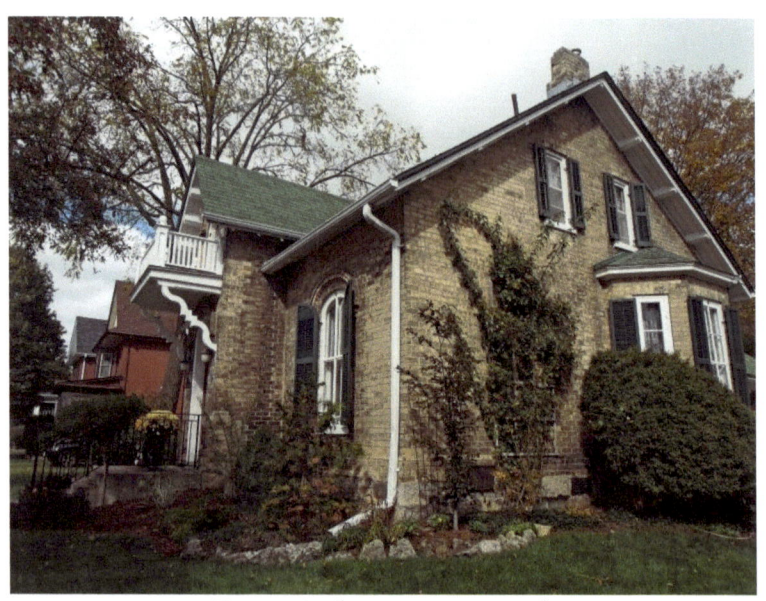

Bay window on one end

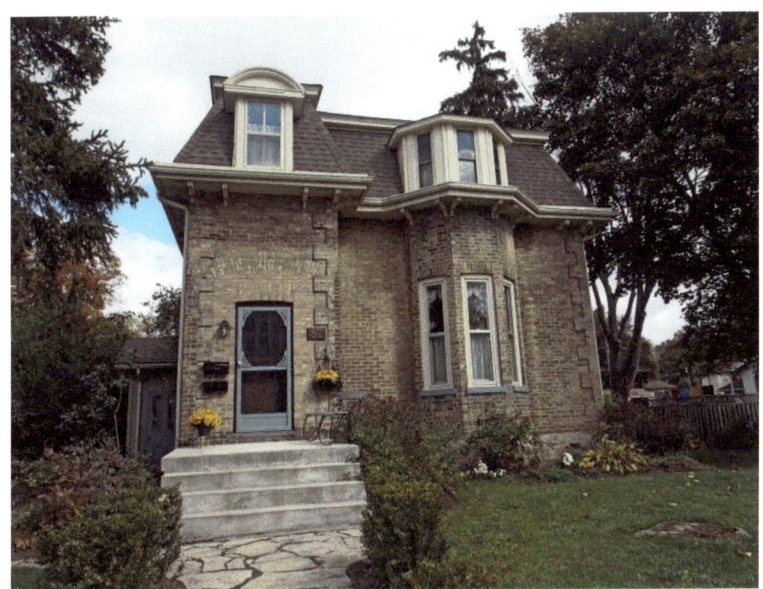

87 Willow Street – Second Empire style – mansard roof, tall windows, dormers

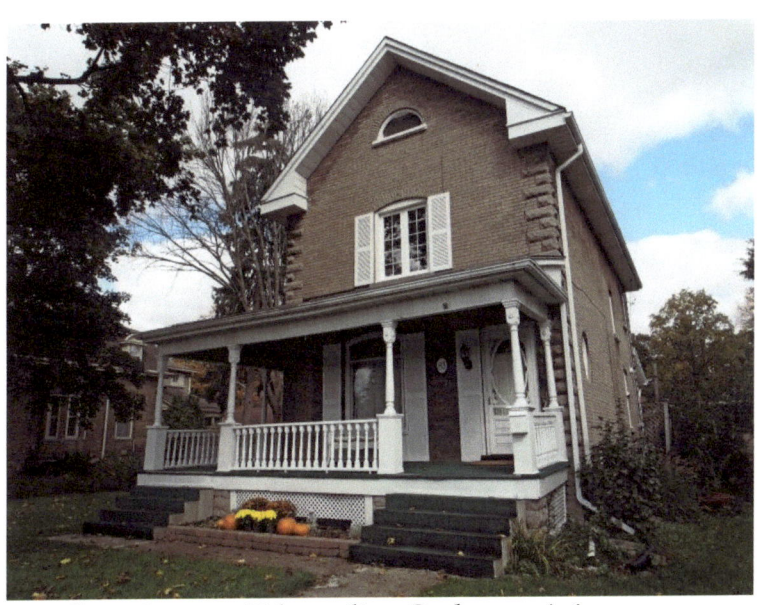

83 Willow Street – Edwardian Style, quoining on corners

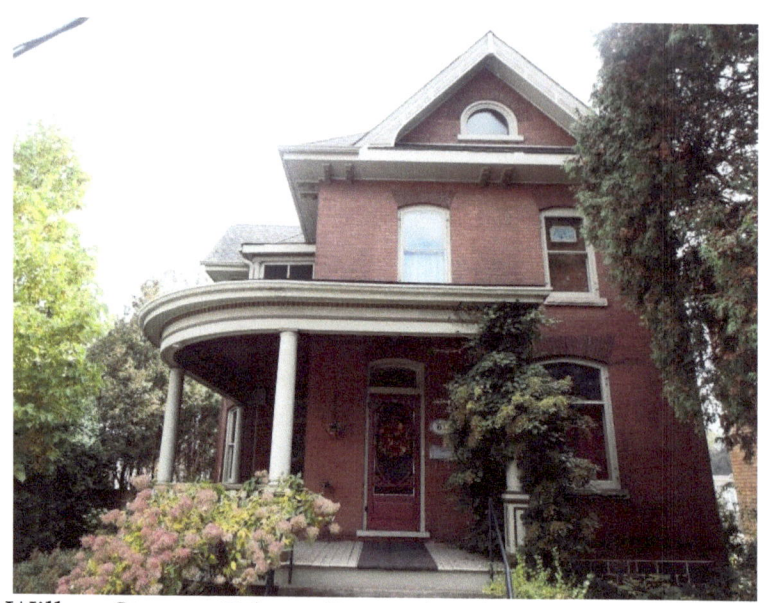

61 Willow Street – Edwardian style – large front wraparound porch, smooth red brick surface

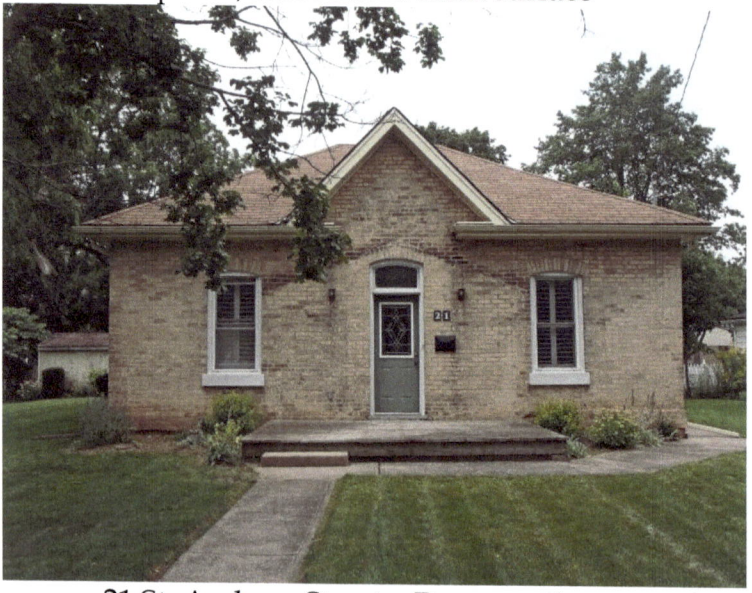

21 St. Andrew Street – Regency Cottage

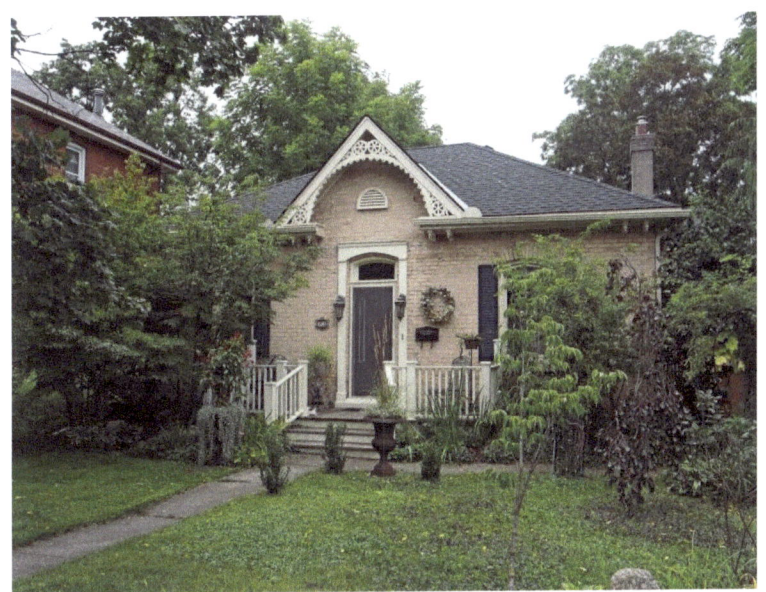

23 St. Andrew Street – Gothic – verge board trim on gable, transom window (fanlight)

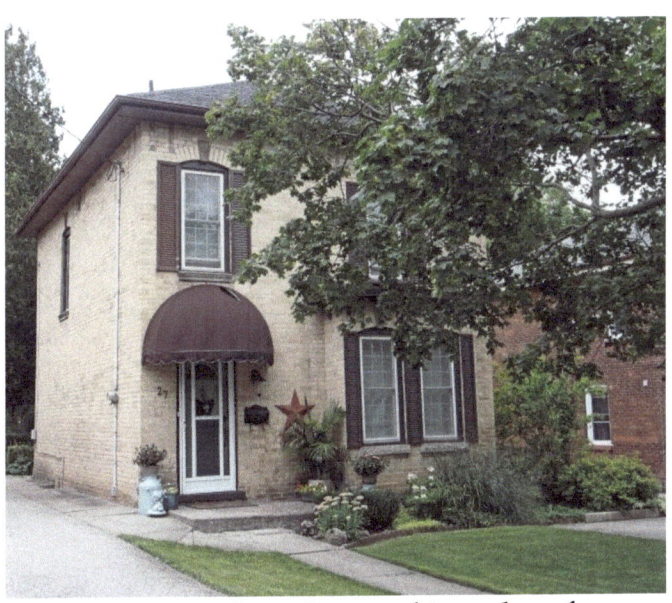

27 St. Andrew Street – hipped roof

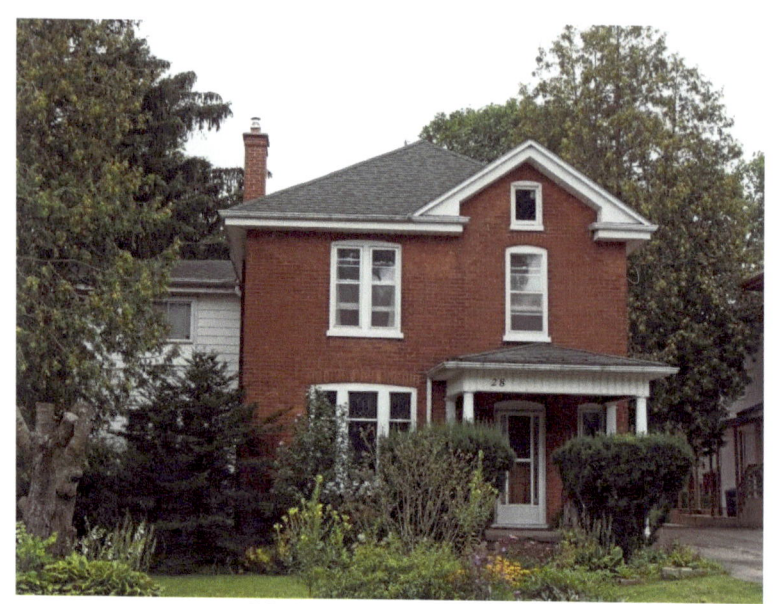

28 St. Andrew Street

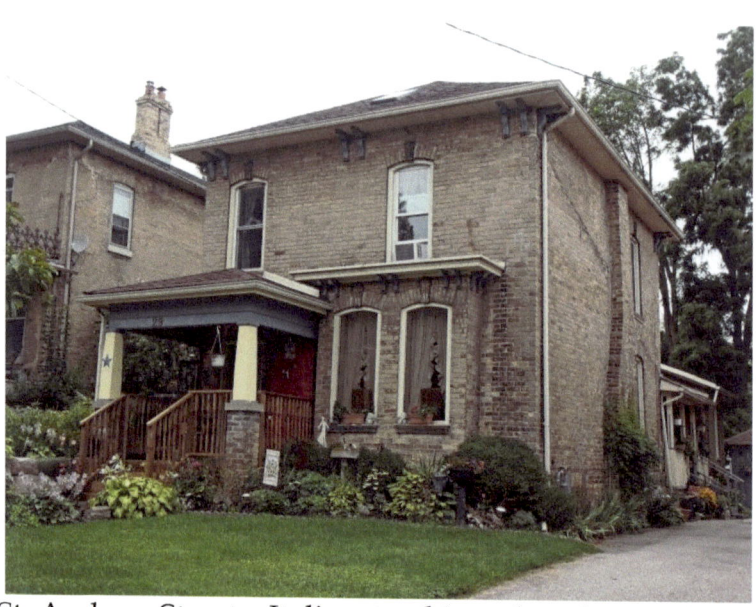

29 St. Andrew Street – Italianate - hipped roof, paired cornice brackets, rectangular bay window

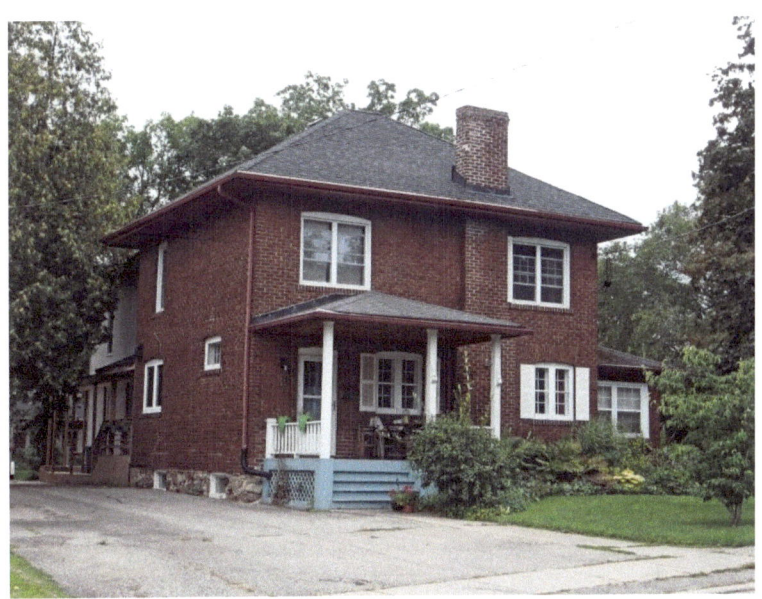

30 St. Andrew Street – hipped roof

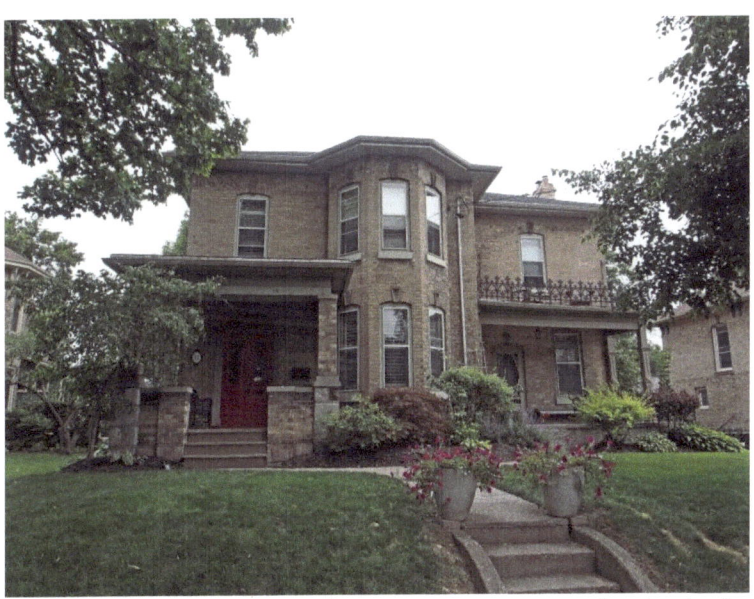

31 St. Andrew Street – Italianate – two-storey bay window, voussoirs and keystones, iron cresting around balcony

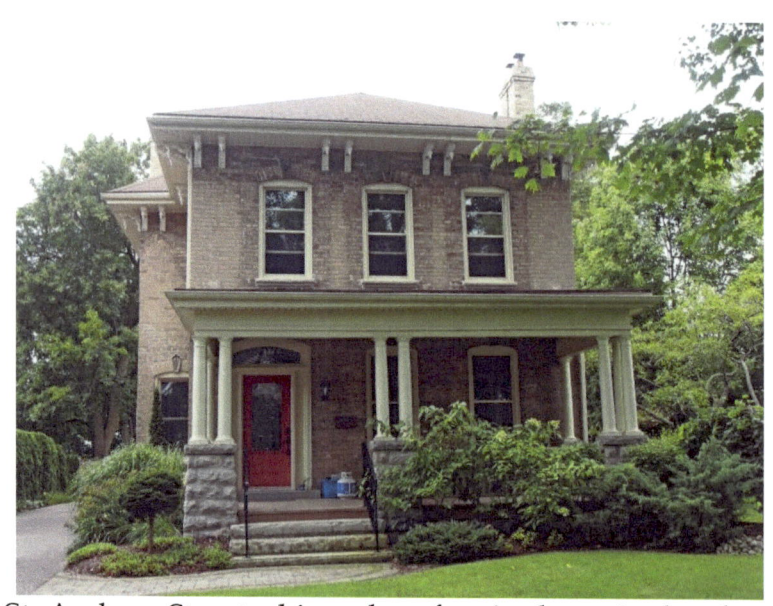

St. Andrew Street – hipped roof, paired cornice brackets

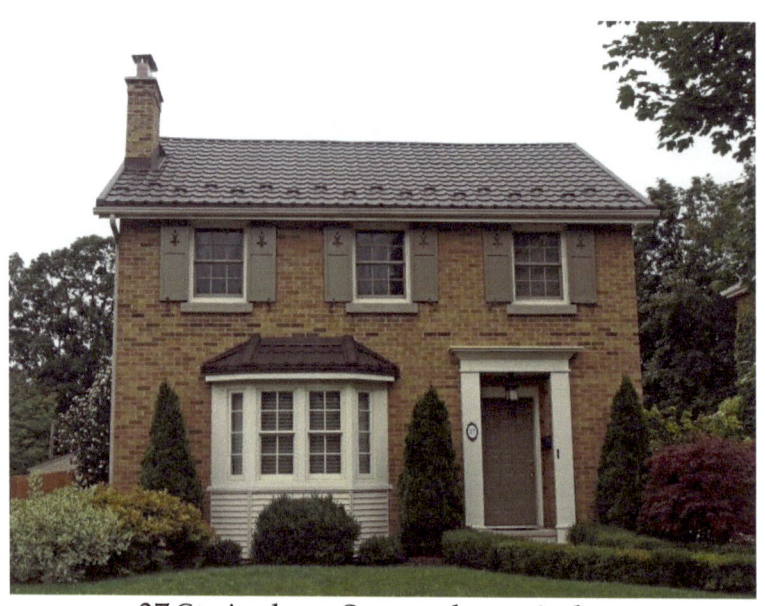

37 St. Andrew Street – bay window

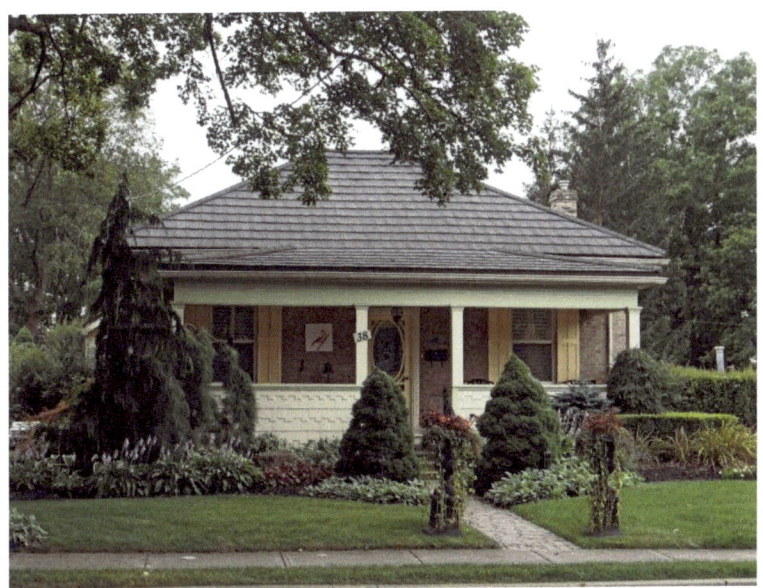

38 St. Andrew Street

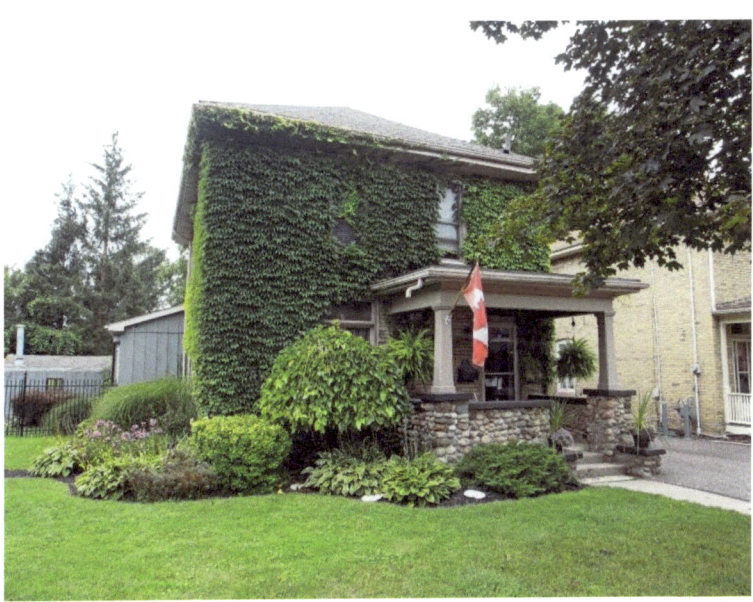

40 St. Andrew Street – vines are even covering the windows; cobblestone verandah

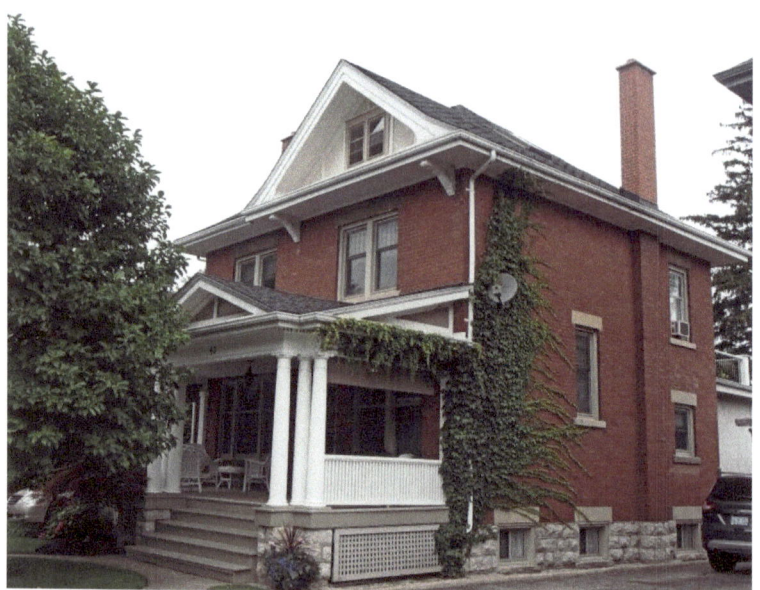

43 St. Andrew Street - Edwardian

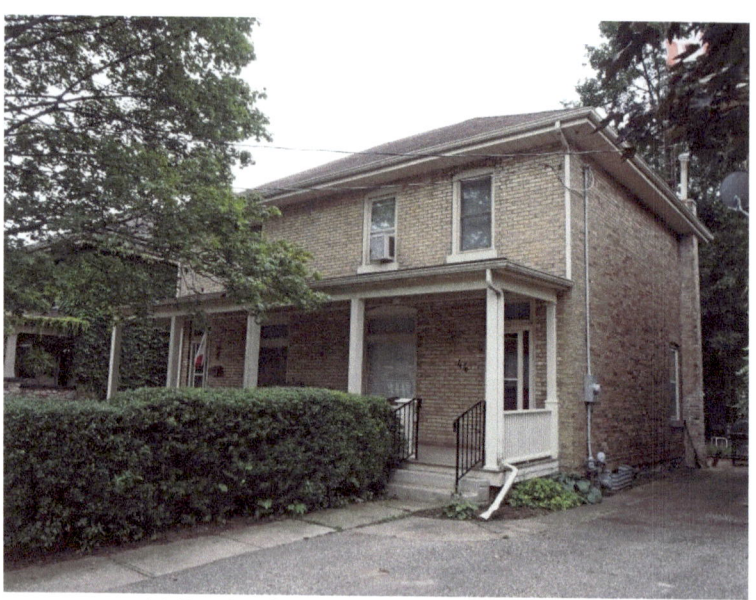

44 St. Andrew Street – hipped roof

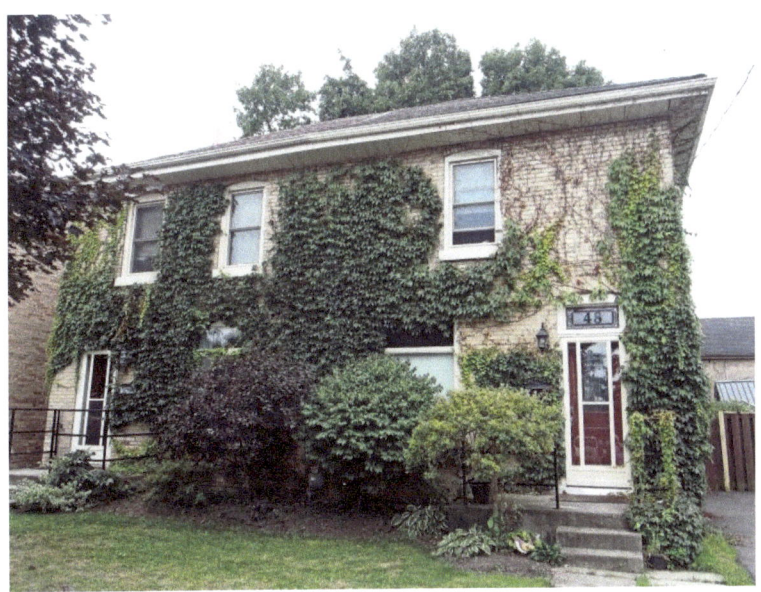
46-48 St. Andrew Street – fanlight above door

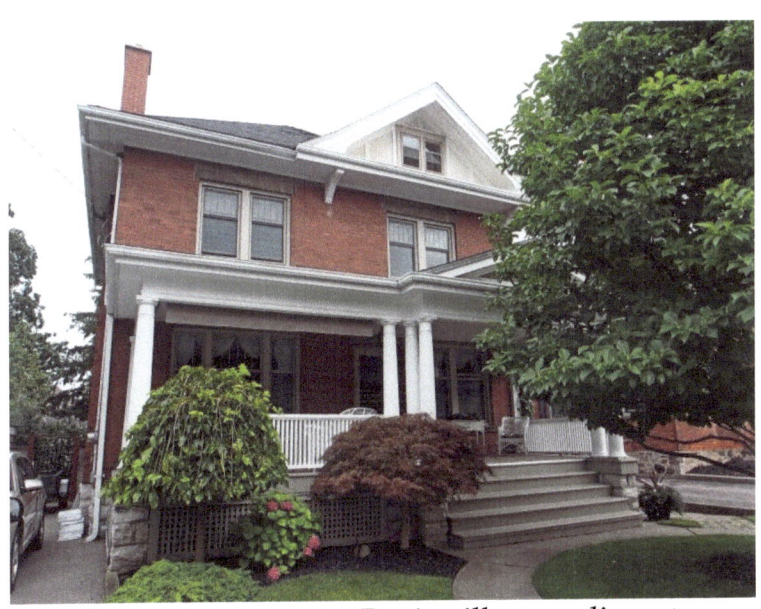
St. Andrew Street – Doric pillars, pediment

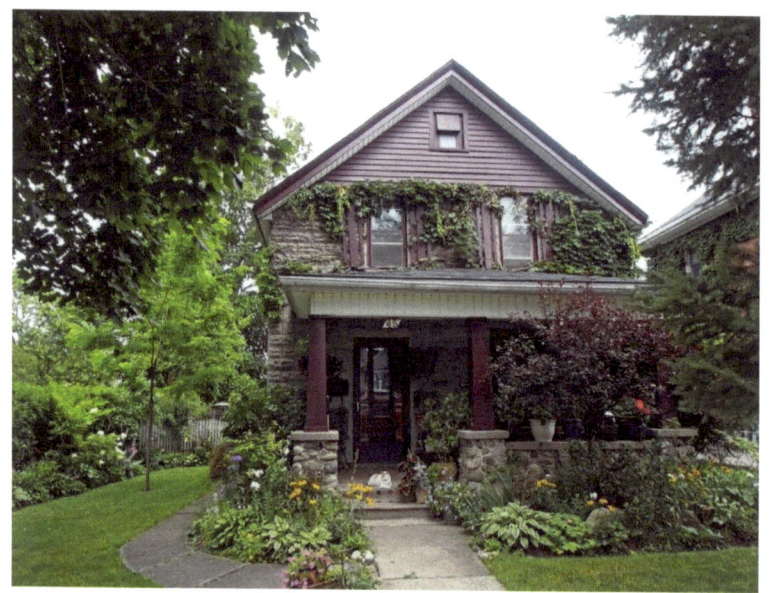
45 St. Andrew Street

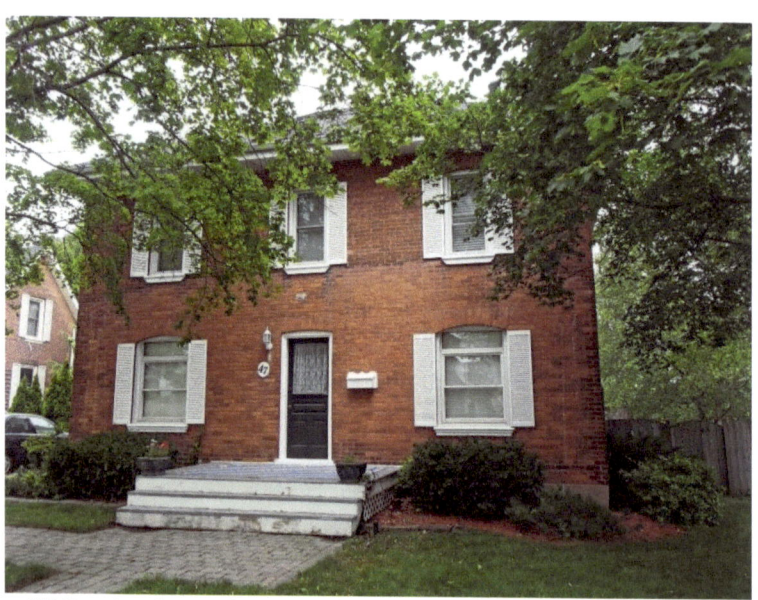
47 St. Andrew Street – hipped roof, balanced façade

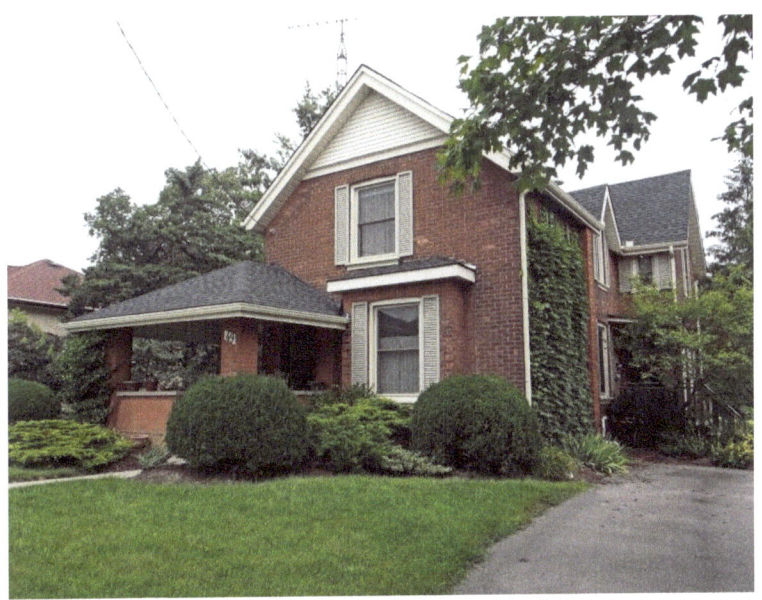

49 St. Andrew Street - Gothic

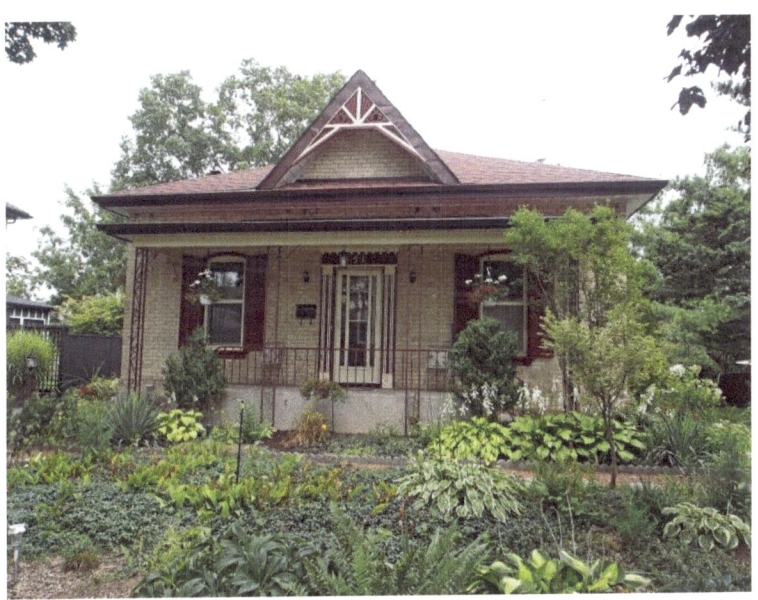

51 St. Andrew Street – Regency Cottage

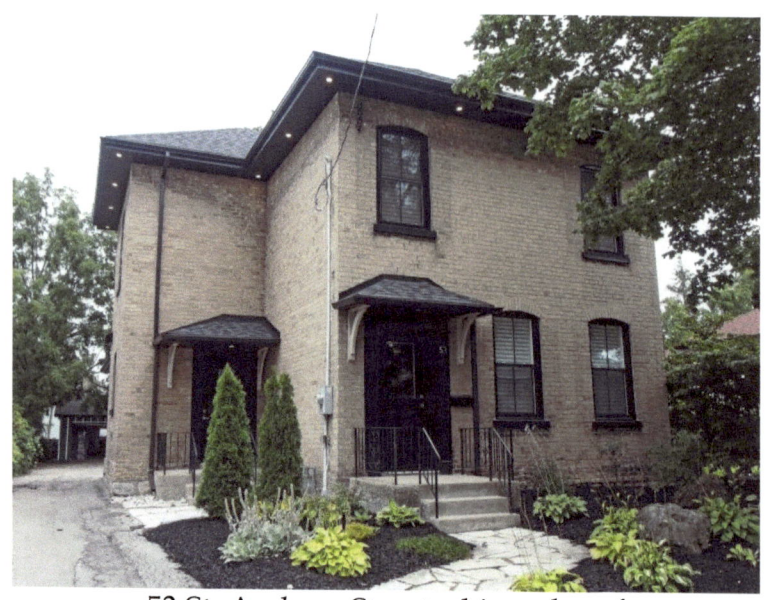
53 St. Andrew Street – hipped roof

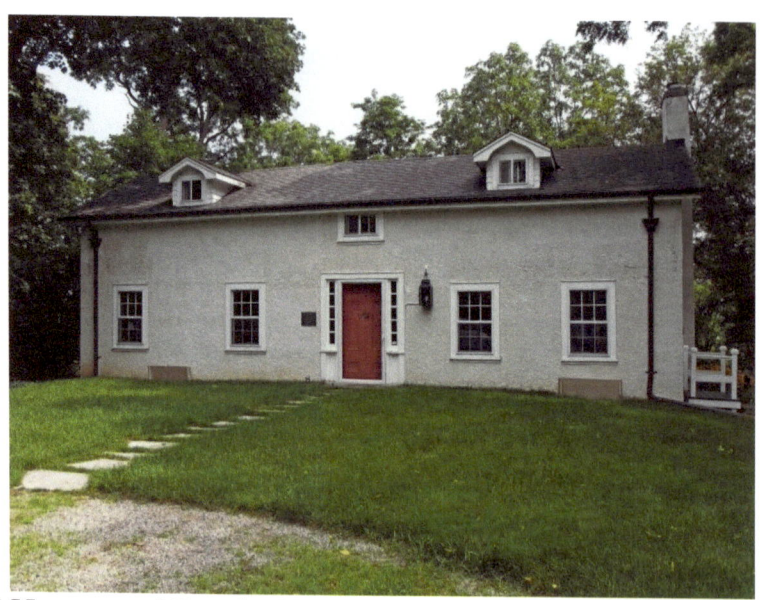
8 Homestead Road – Hiram Capron House built in 1831 – plastered frame house

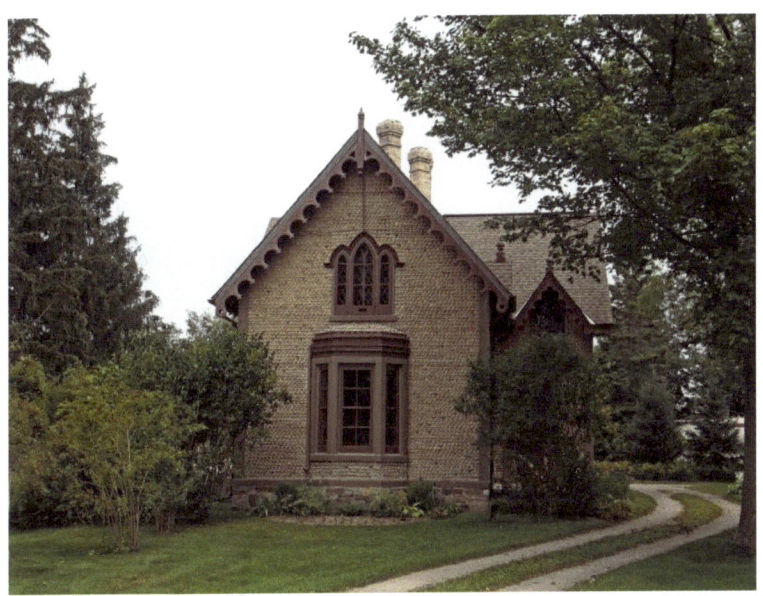

33 Oak Avenue – 1854 – built by David Patton and his wife Matilda (Killips) Patton – 1½-storey Gothic Revival style of cobblestone and fieldstone construction. The main façade gable is decorated with gingerbread and has a set of Gothic windows. Three walls are cobblestone and the rear of the house is of cut stone.

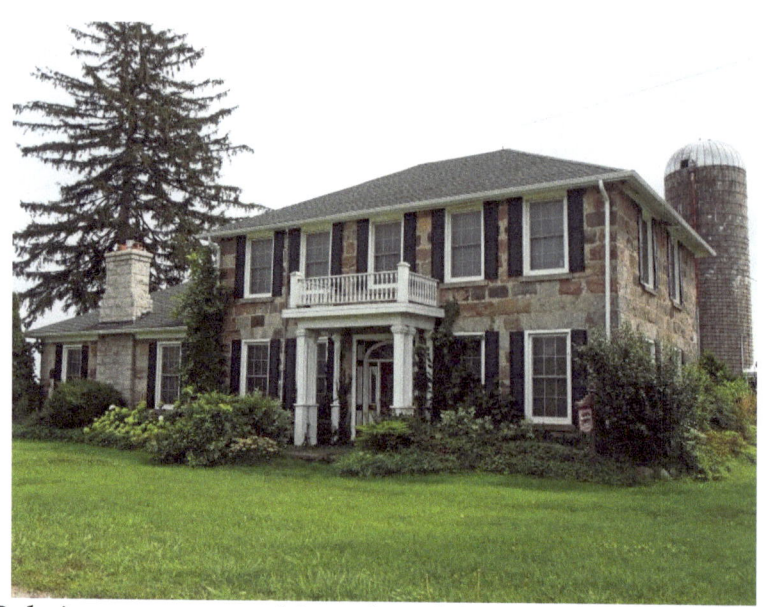

Oak Avenue – stone, hipped roof, balcony above entrance

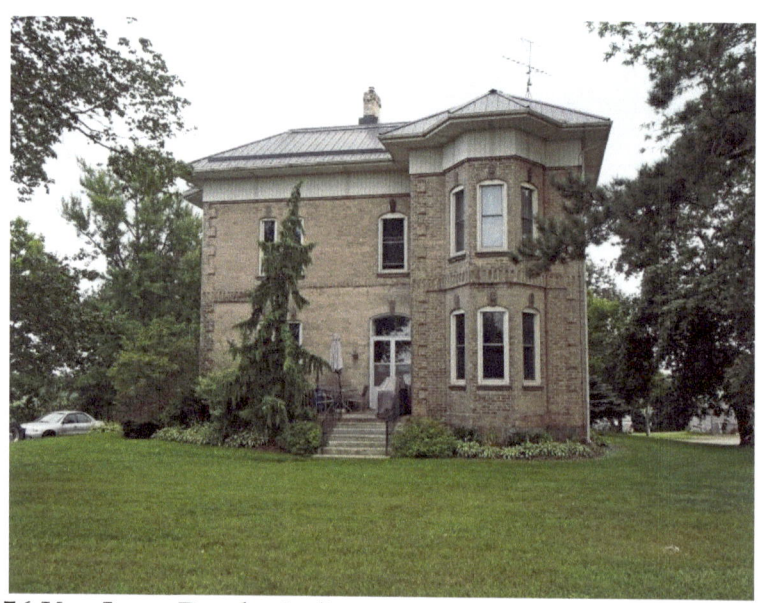

956 Keg Lane Road – Italianate – two-storey bay window, corner quoins

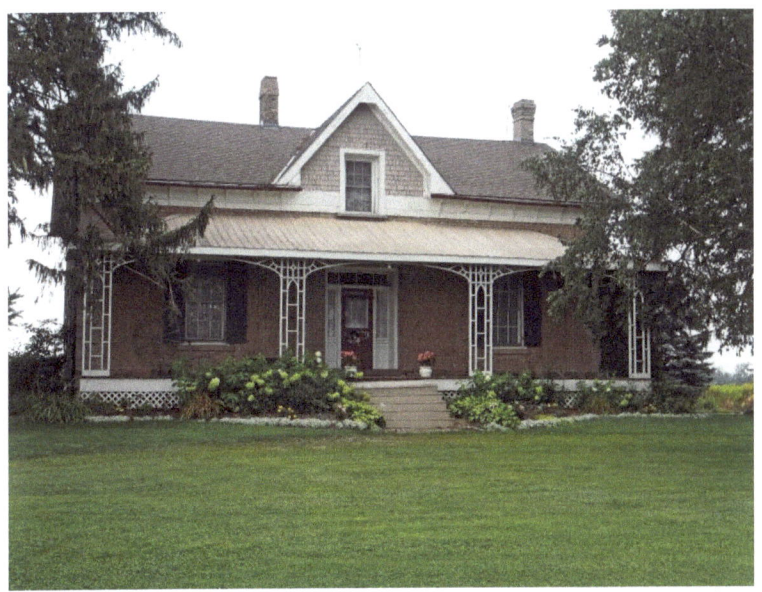

963 Keg Lane Road – The Deans family of 6 first lived in a single-storey log cabin on the corner of the property. After 7 more children arrived, construction began on this house. In 1862 construction was completed with cobblestone walls on three sides. The trellised stone verandah closely matches the original one; all the shutters are original.

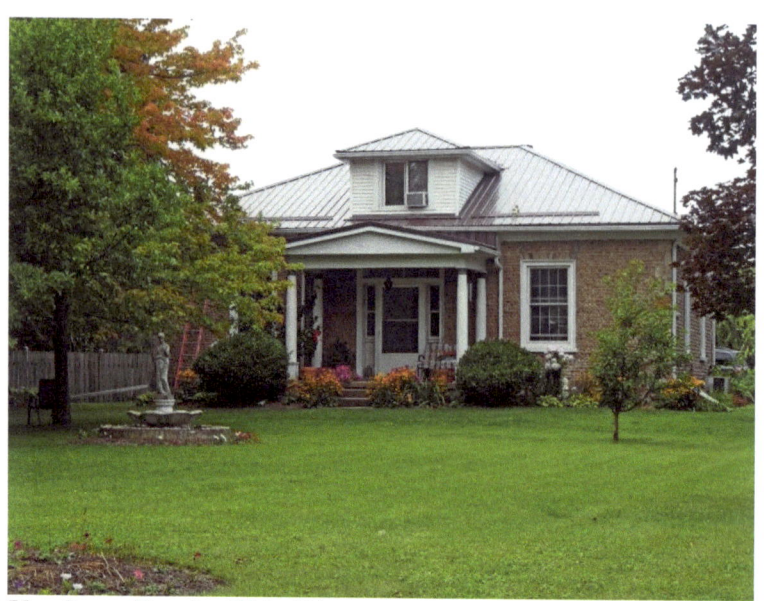

899 Keg Lane Road – This 1½ storey Regency Style house with four cobblestone walls was built for Charles and Margaret O'Neail, circa 1861, by his father Daniel O'Neail who came to Canada from Ireland in 1830. Daniel was the first president of the Paris Agricultural Society; Charles later served as president.

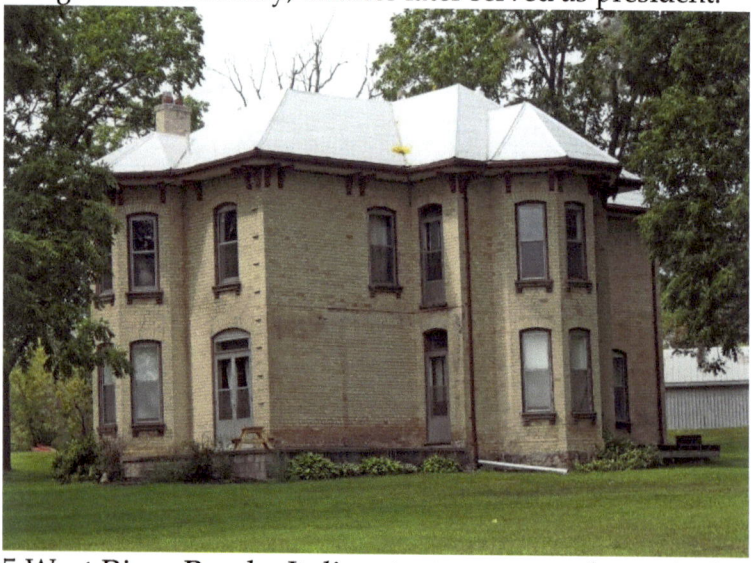

135 West River Road – Italianate, two-storey bay windows, cornice brackets

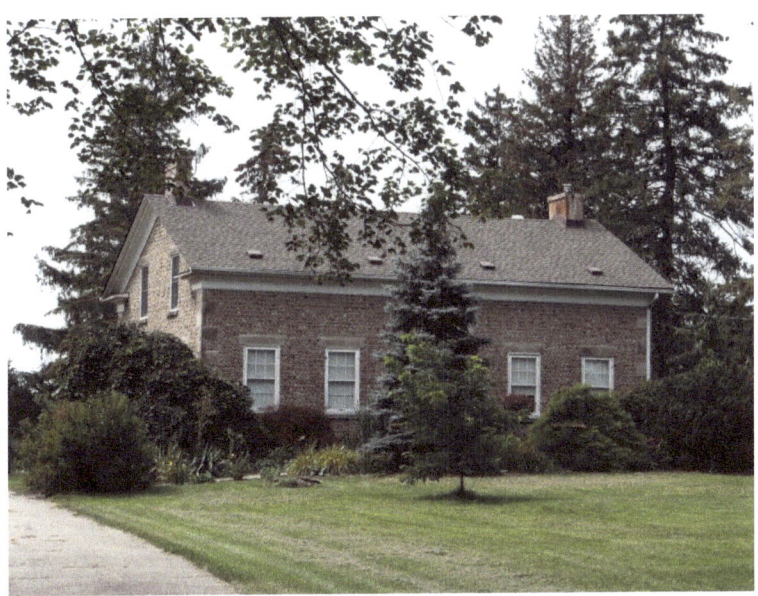

207 West River Road – George Brown residence - Construction began in 1854 and was completed in 1862 – it took years to accumulate all the matching cobblestones. It is reflective of the traditional Ontario Cottage style in the Revival tradition.

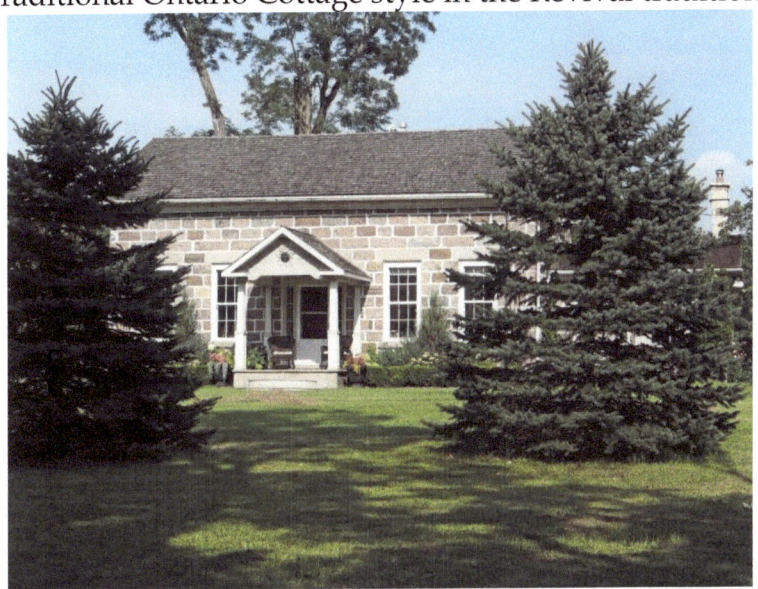

286 West River Road

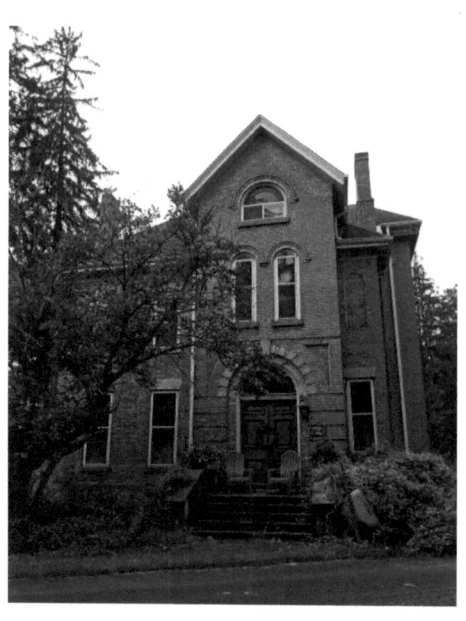

71 Kitchen School Road – Italianate – 2½-storey frontispiece, half-round windows, voussoirs and keystone, transom window above door

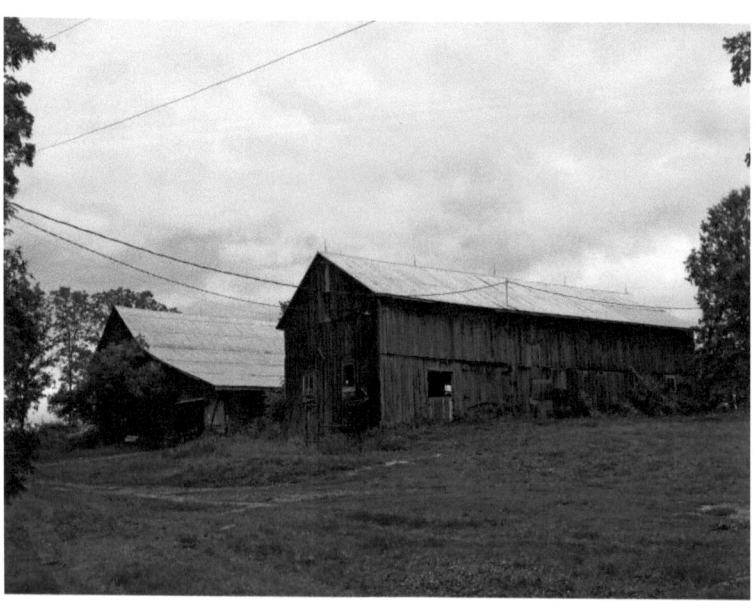

Harrisburg

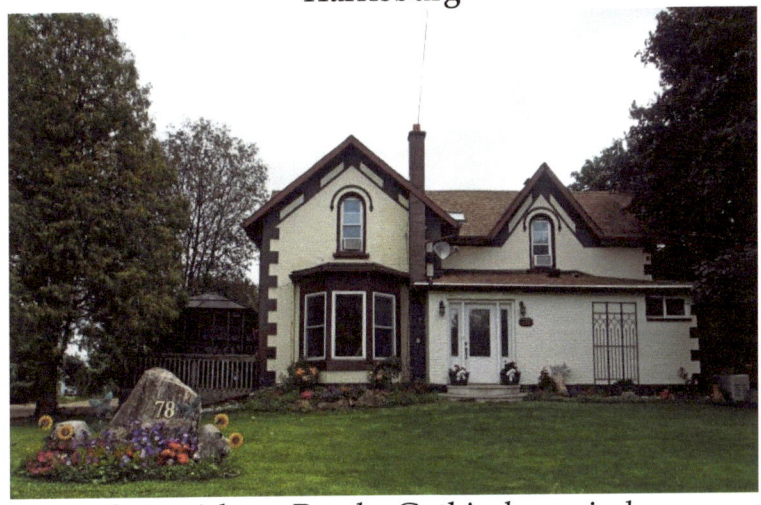

78 Harrisburg Road – Gothic, bay window

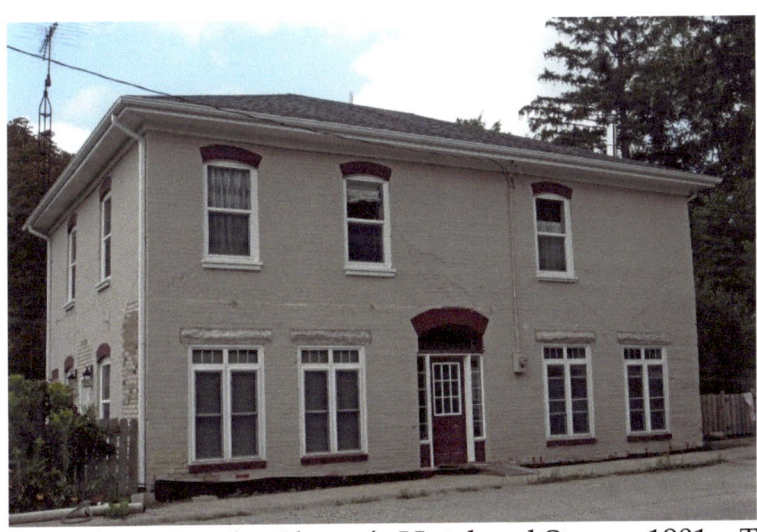

97 Harrisburg Road – Cherry's Hotel and Store – 1901 – This two-storey brick hotel offered rooms, meals and a full service bar. It was later converted to a general store and the Harrisburg Post Office. Mr. and Mrs. A. Norman purchased and operated the store until 1978.

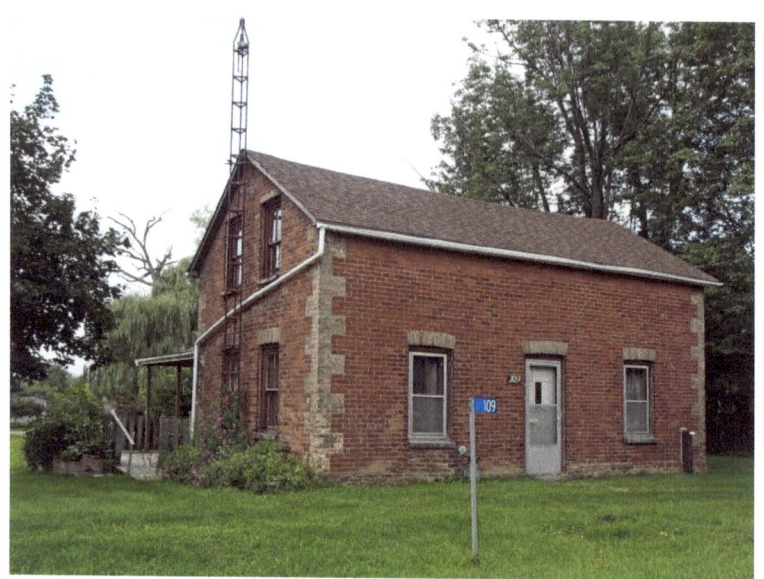

109 Harrisburg Road – Georgian style – 1890 – red brick with contrasting white brick accents, white brick quoins

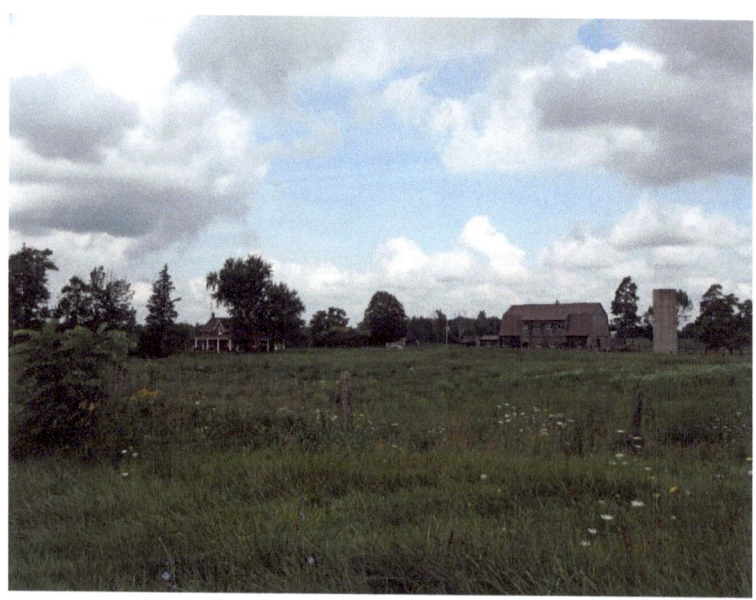

Farm

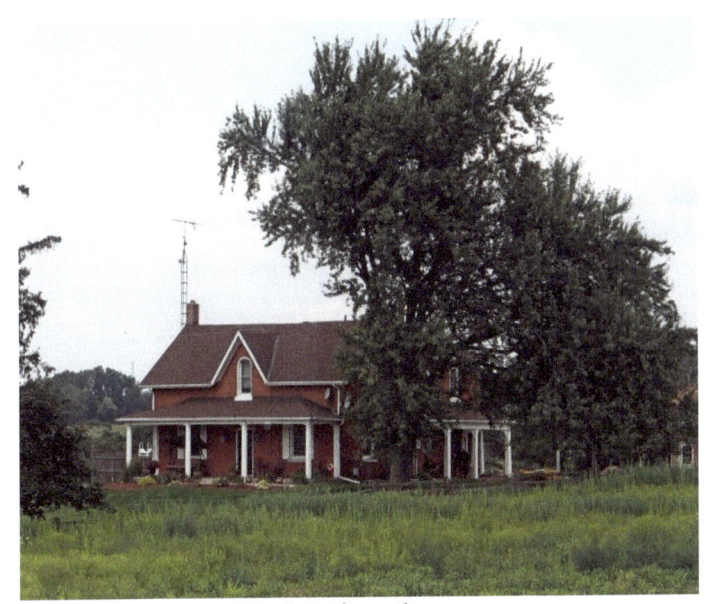

Gothic farmhouse

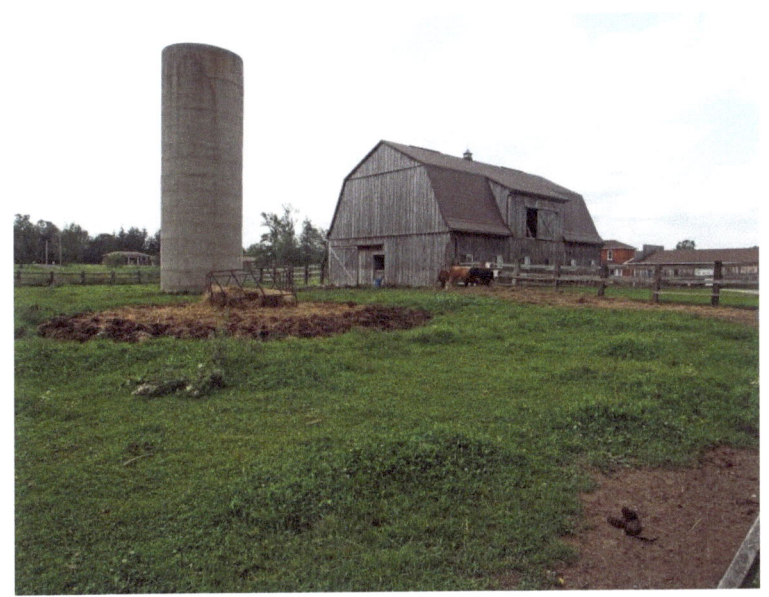

Gambrel roof on barn

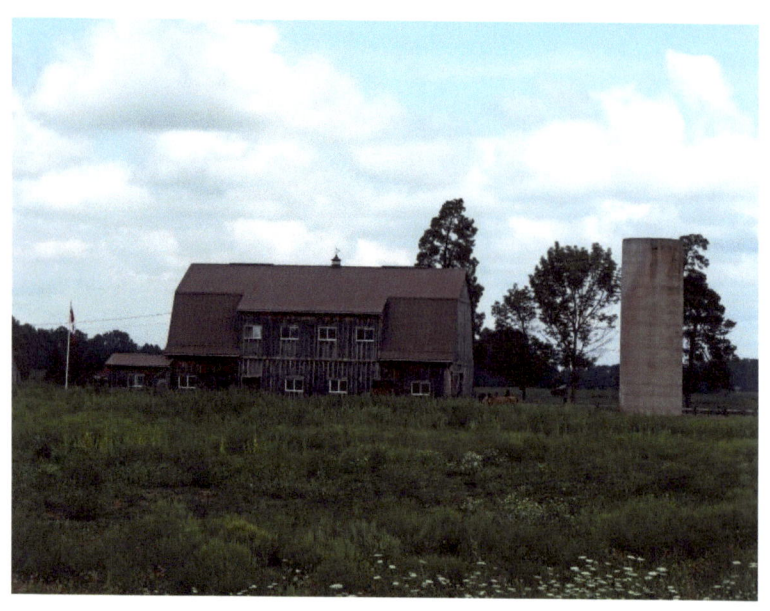

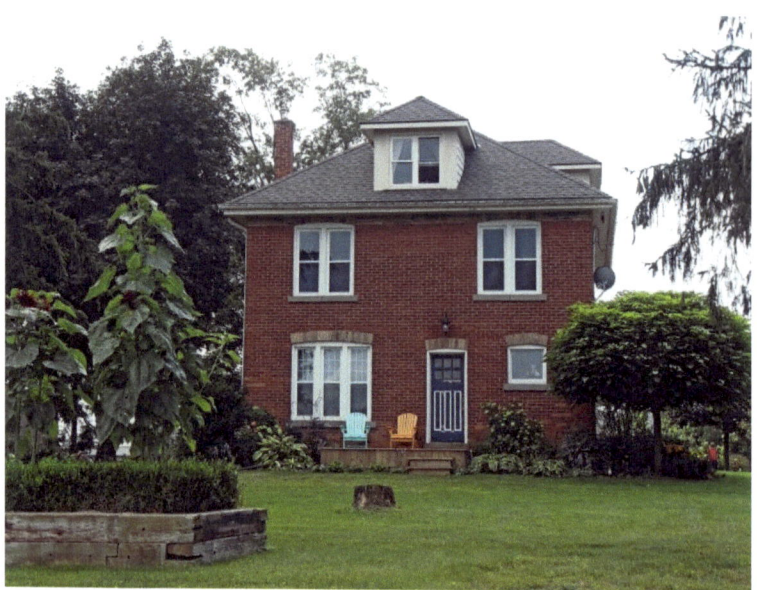

96 German School Road, Brant County 33 – hipped roof, dormers, bay window

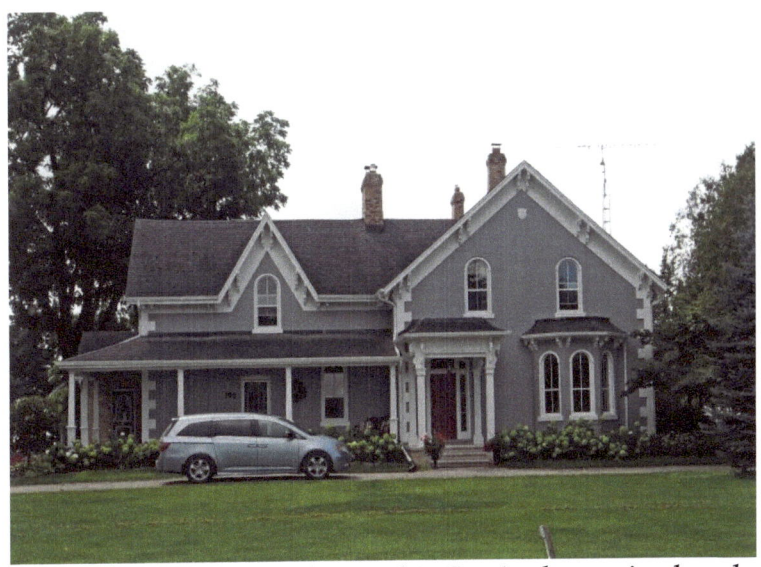

100 German School Road – Gothic Revival, cornice brackets, bay window, corner quoins

Glen Morris

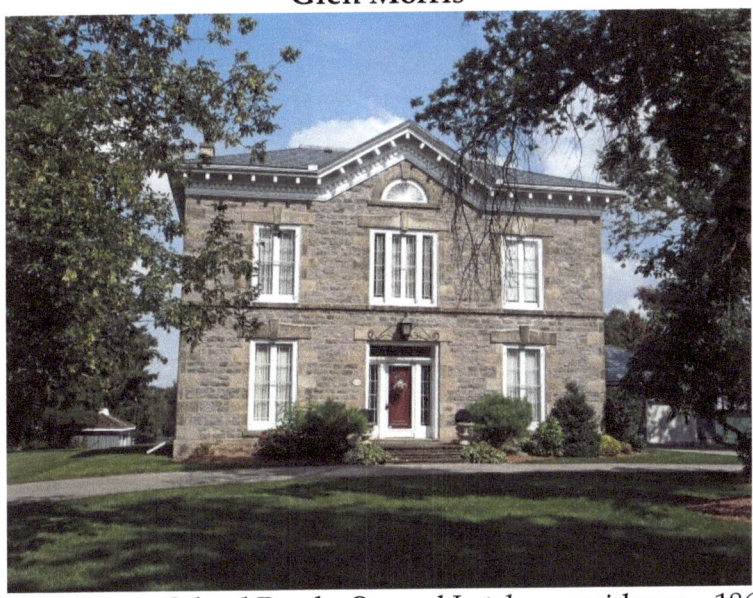

448 McPherson School Road – Samuel Latshaw residence – 1860 – The walls are made of rubble stone with cut stone around the windows.

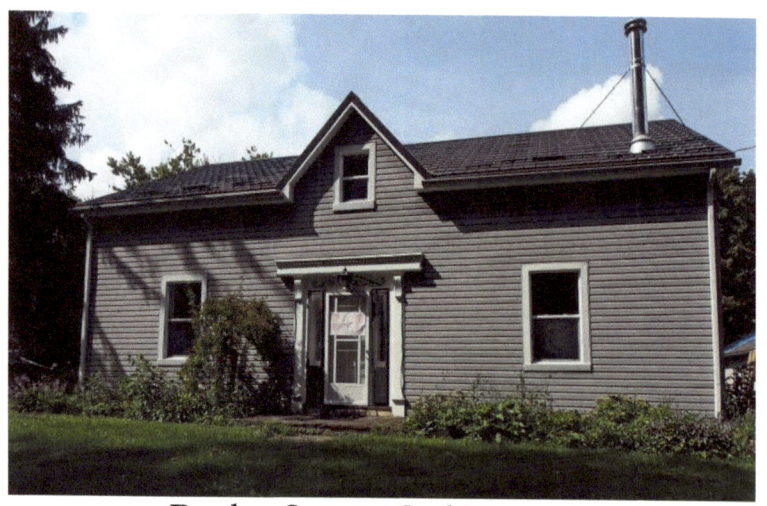

Dunbar Street – Gothic cottage

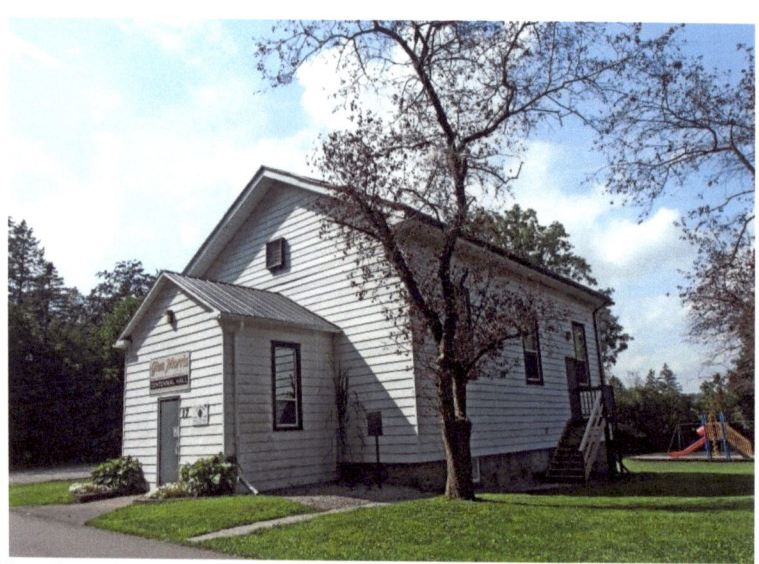

17 Dunbar Street – circa 1860 – Originally built as a Methodist Church – purchased for the Women's Institute in 1912. From 1955-1961 it was used as a school. Today it is used as a community meeting place.

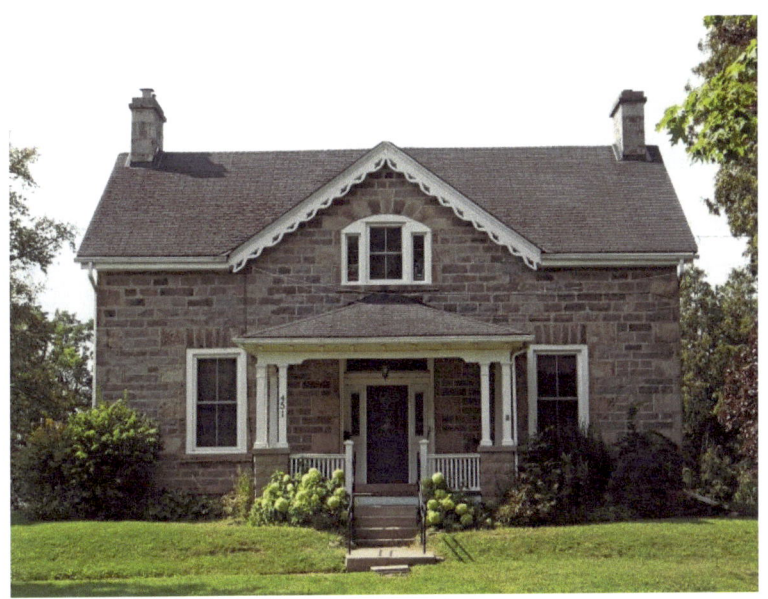

451 East River Road – Gothic style

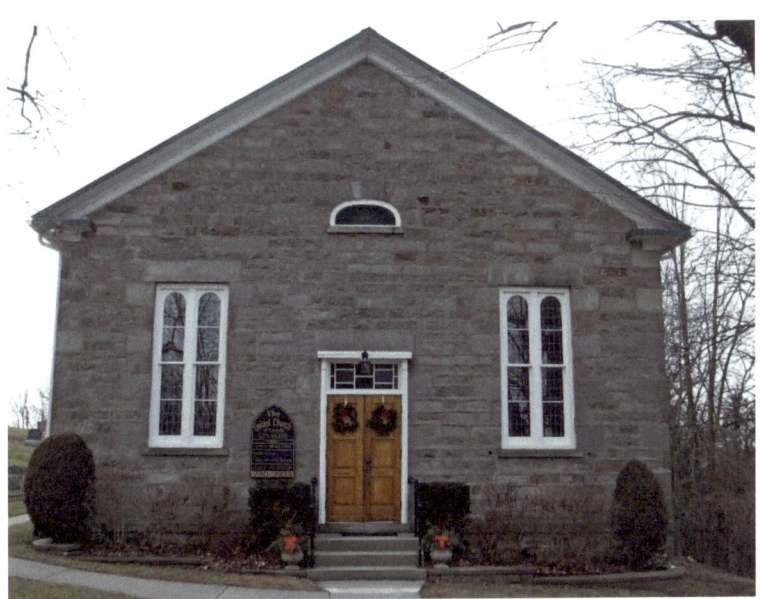

453 East River Road – Glen Morris United Church

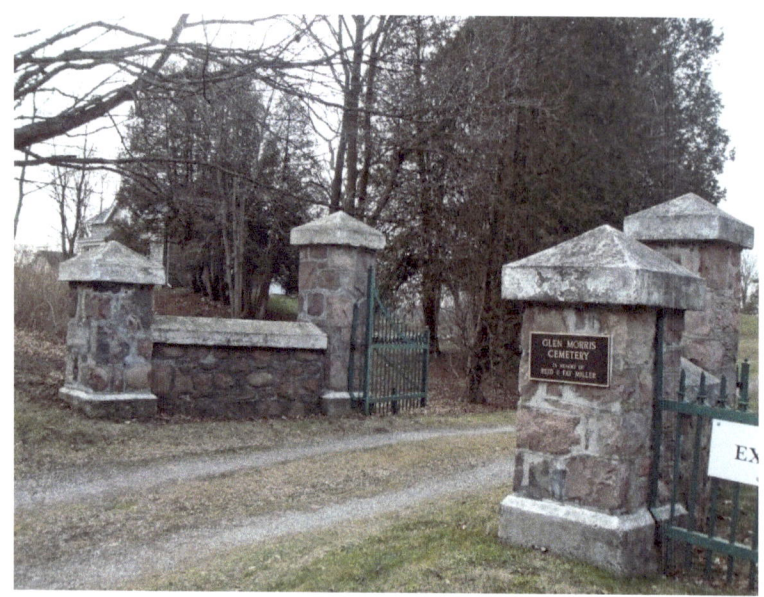
East River Road – Glen Morris Cemetery Gates

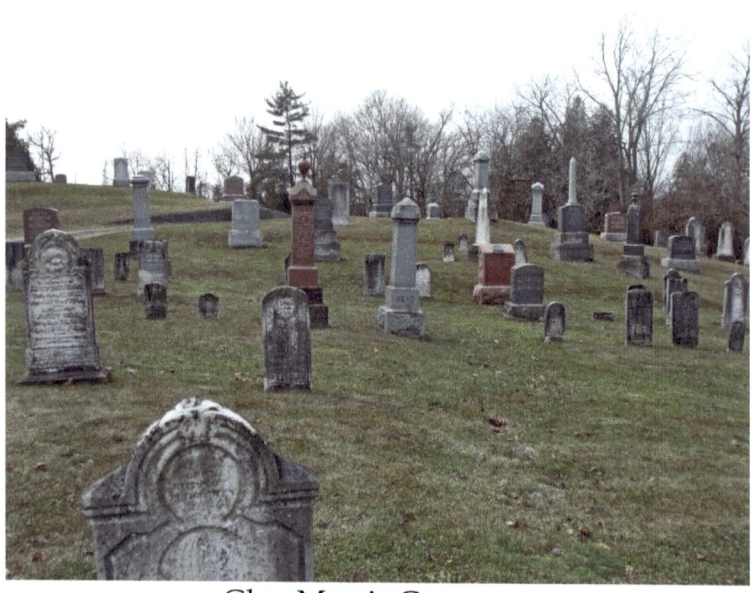
Glen Morris Cemetery

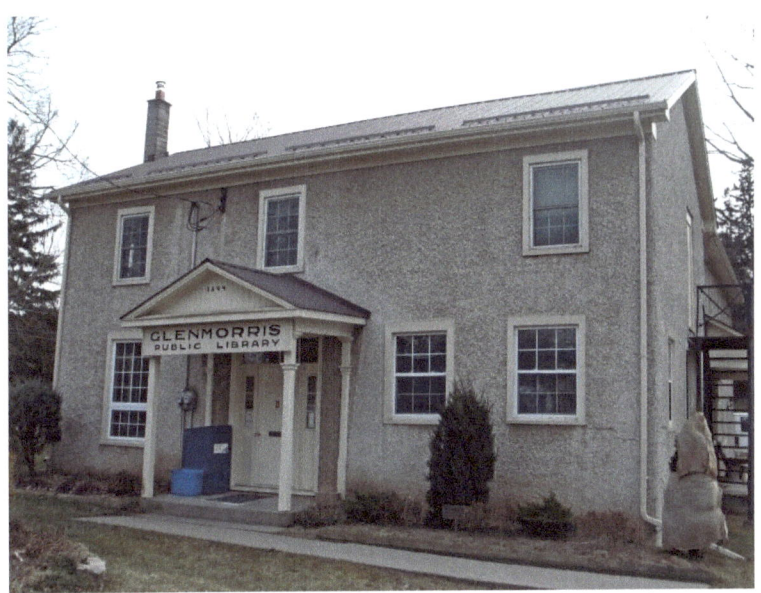

474 East River Road – Glen Morris Public Library

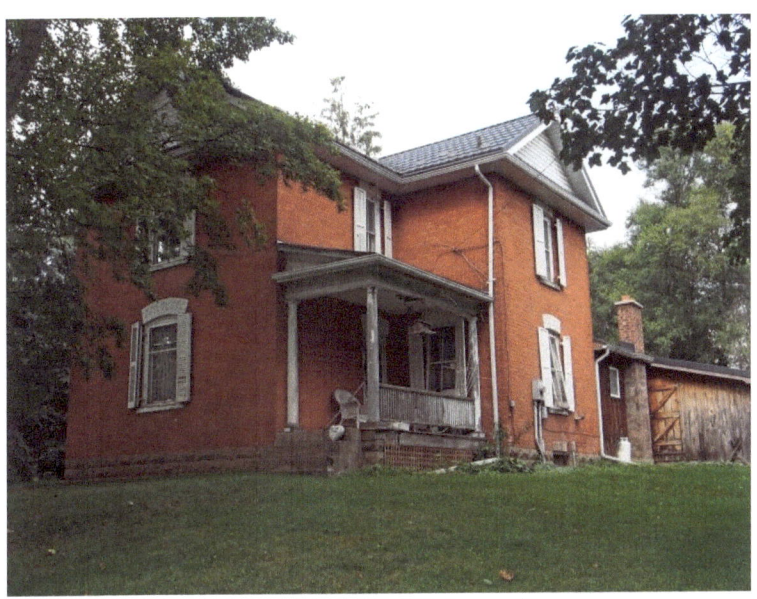

Princess Street - Edwardian

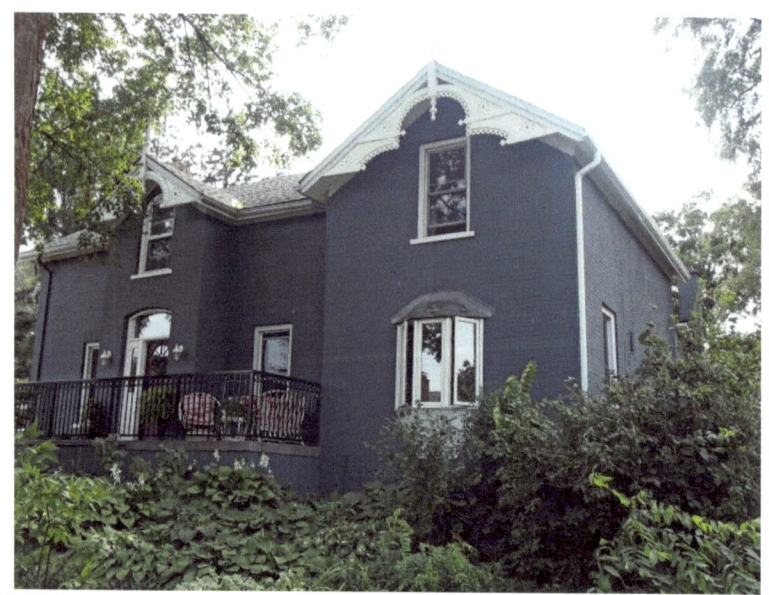

23 Princess Street – Gothic Revival – verge board trim and finials on gables, oriel window

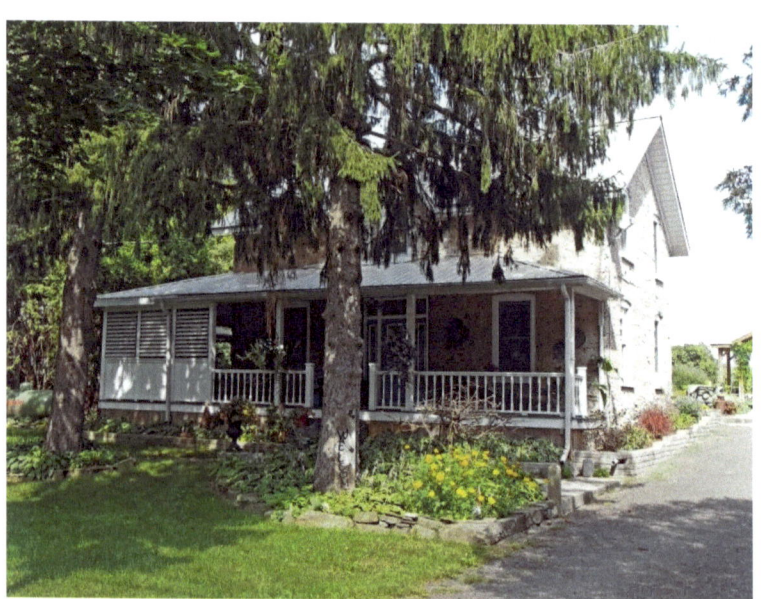

Princess Street

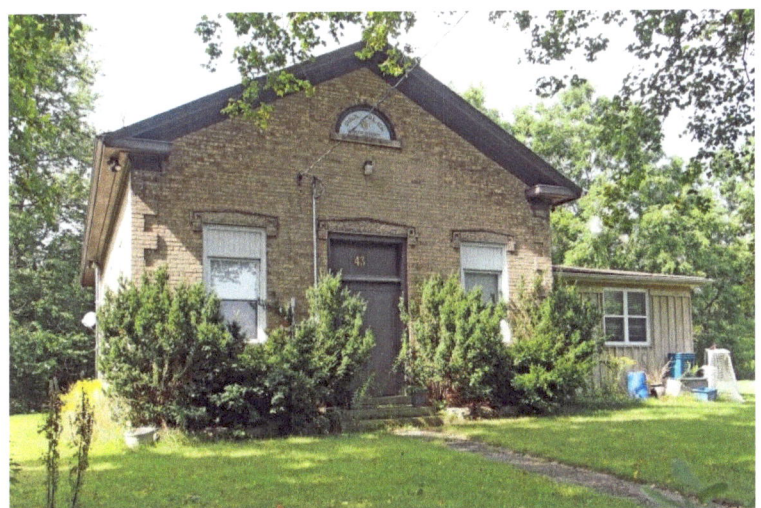

43 Princess Street – Glen Morris School, S.S. No. 14 – 1835 – built on land donated by Christopher Latshaw. The school is now used by the Preston District Girl Guides.

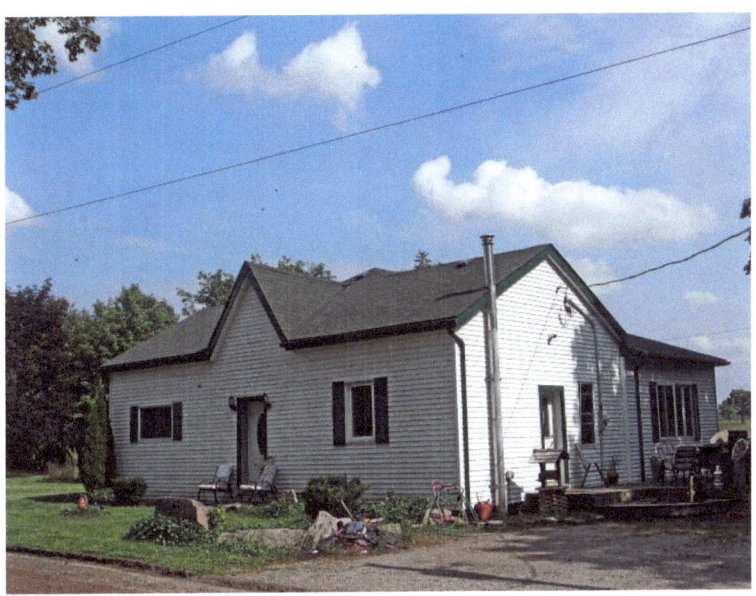

Princess Street - Gothic

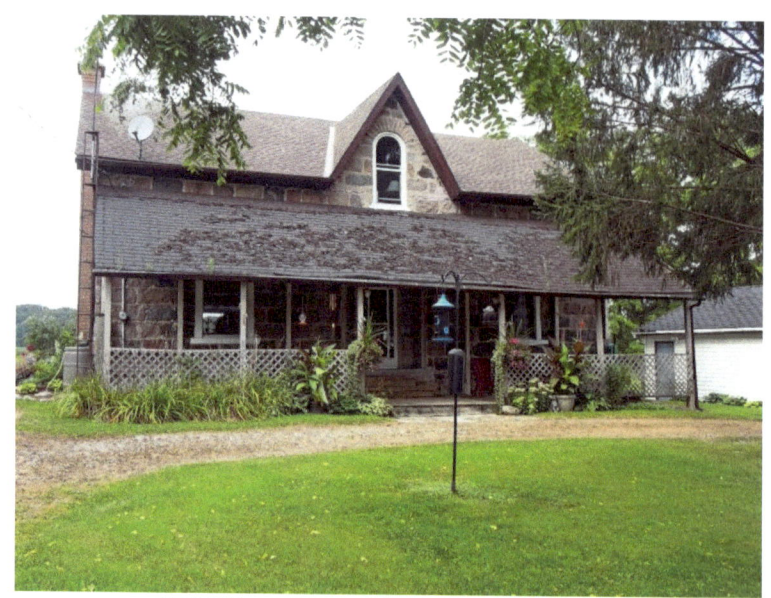

850 West Dumfries Road - Gothic

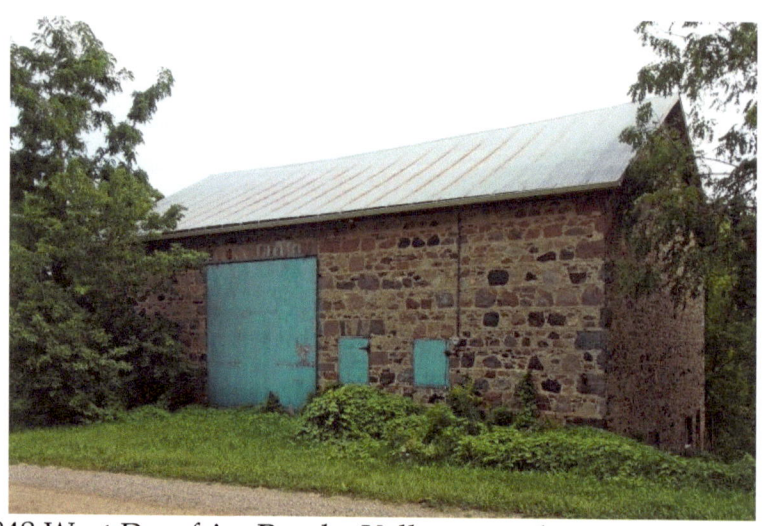

848 West Dumfries Road – Kelley stone barn, circa 1855 – constructed by Scottish masons with fieldstone from the foundation all the way to the roof

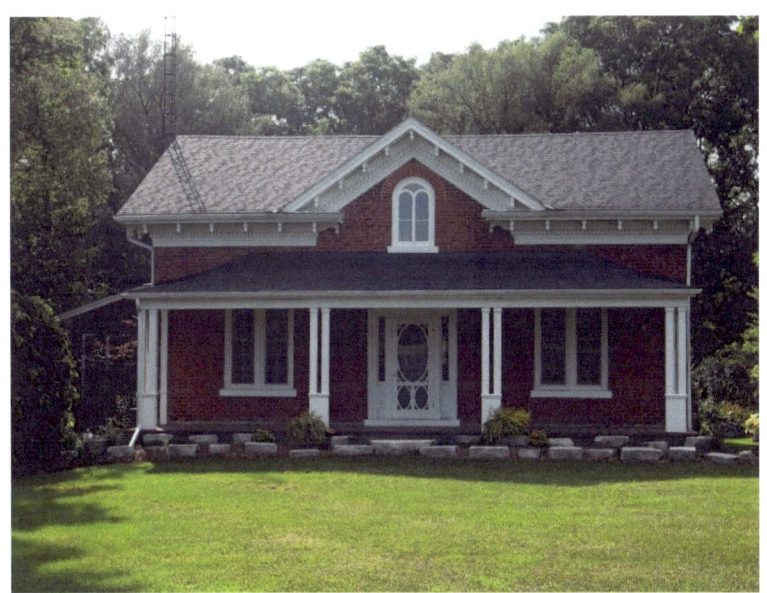

283 Pinehurst Road – Gothic - sidelights

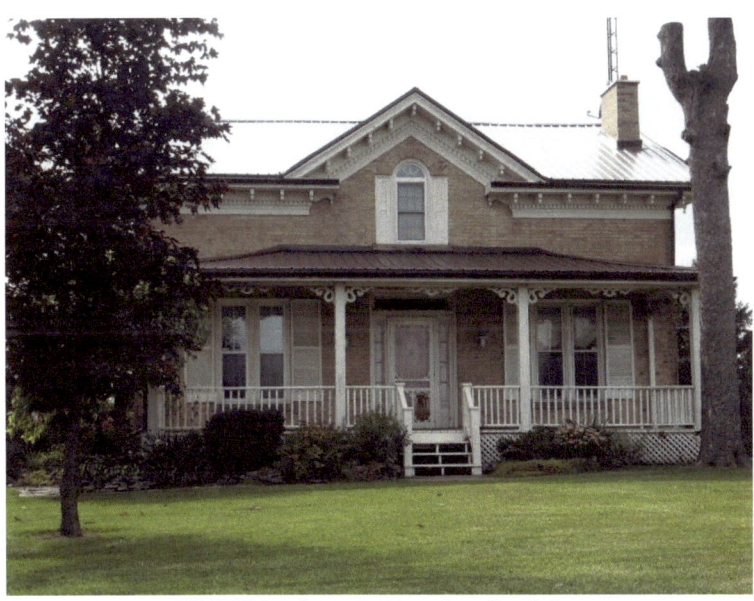

357 Pinehurst Road - Gothic

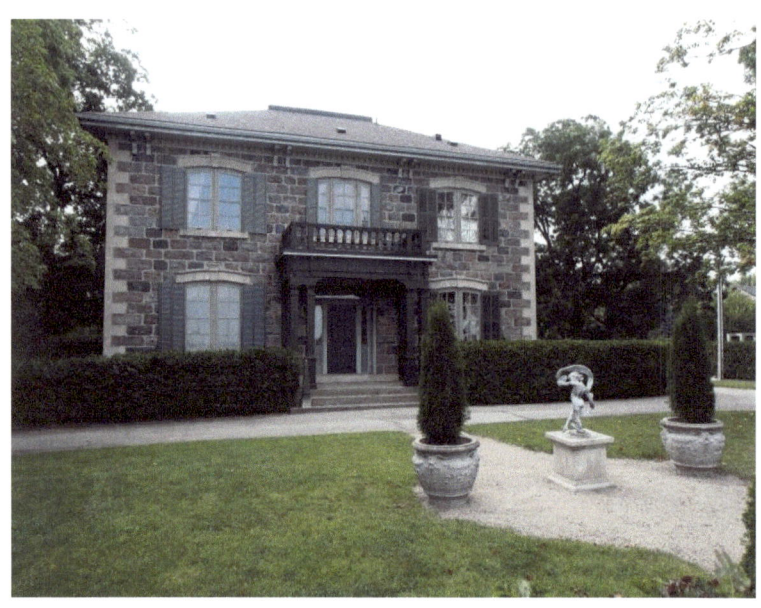

289 Pinehurst Road – This fieldstone house of Provincial Scottish Victorian architecture was built in 1860 for one of the early settlers in this area, John Maus. The stone for this farmer's residence and carriage house came from local fields.

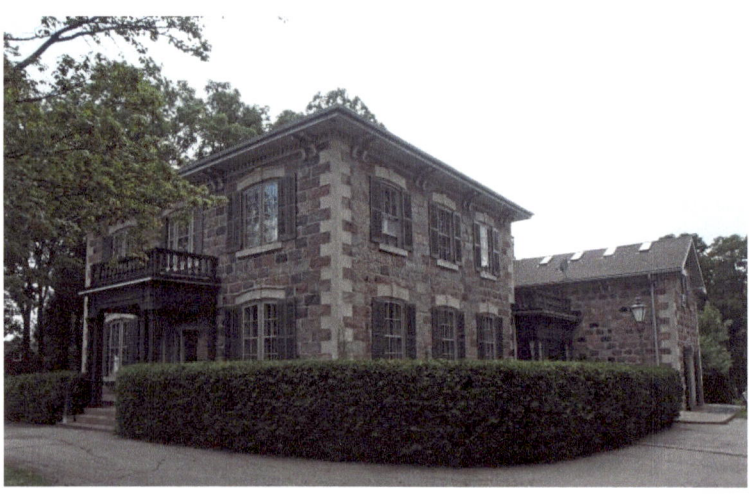

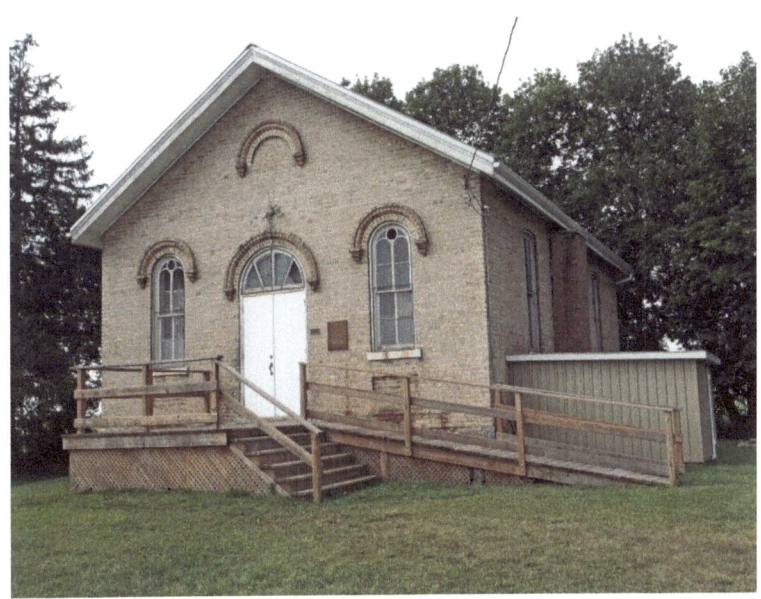

705 Paris Plains Church Road – Maus School, S.S. No. 18 -1847 – The land for this school was donated by Henry Maus. It was converted to a school museum in 1967.

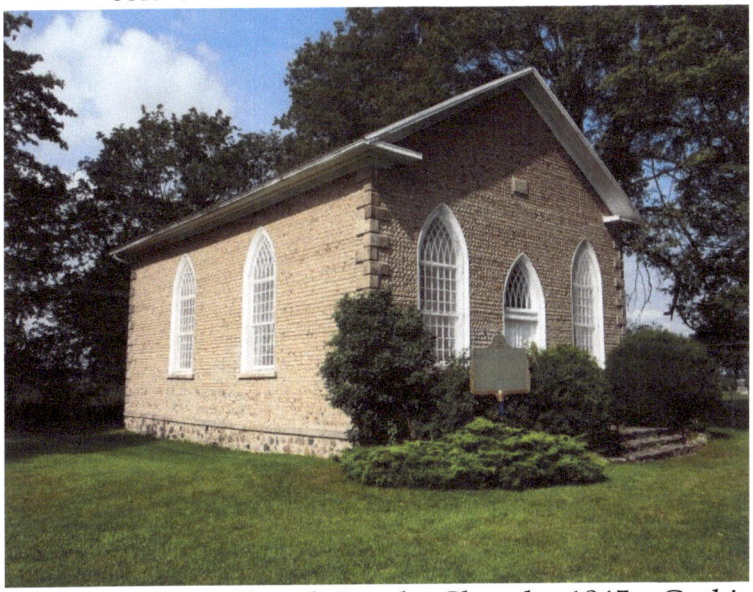

705 Paris Plains Church Road – Church - 1845 – Gothic Revival – cobblestone construction; lancet windows, cornice return on gable

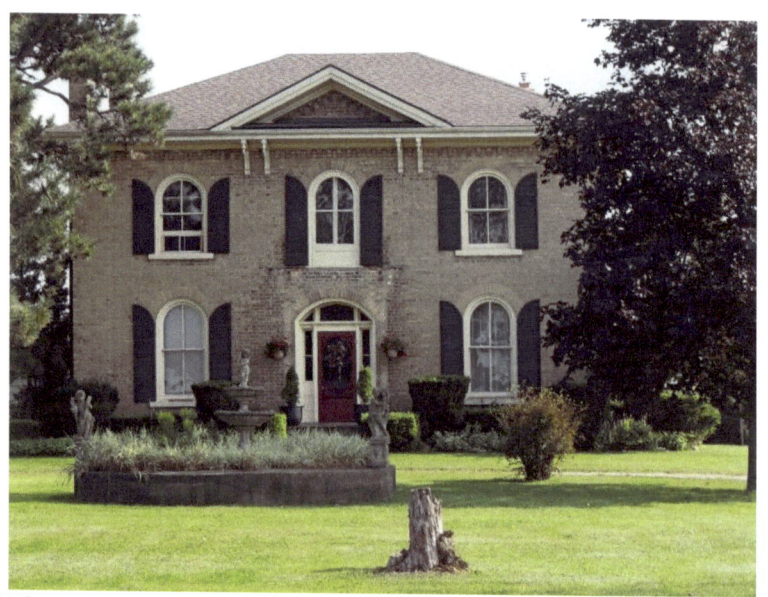

716 Watts Pond Road – Italianate, paired cornice brackets, half-round windows, sidelights and transom windows

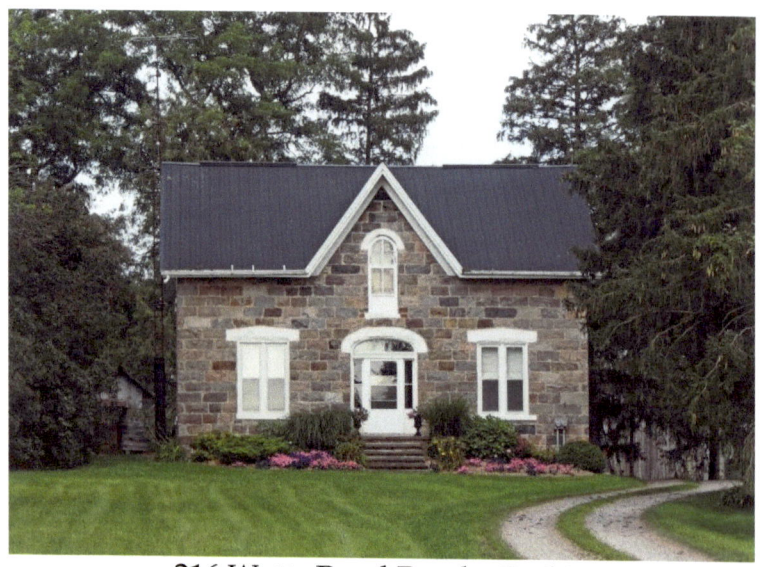

216 Watts Pond Road - Gothic

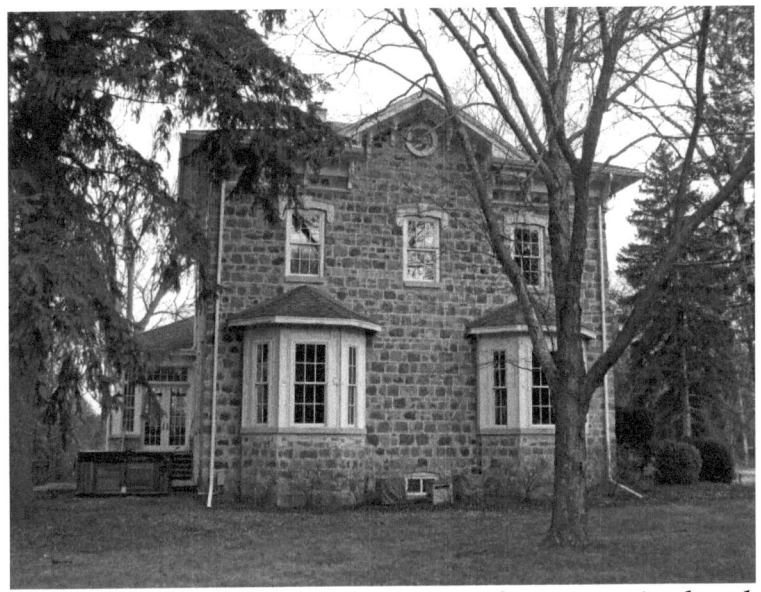

2½-storey – Italianate - stone, bay windows, cornice brackets

Architectural Terms

Bay Window: A window that projects out from a wall, in a semicircular, rectangular, or polygonal design. Used frequently in Gothic and Victorian designs. Example: 33 Oak Avenue, Page 25	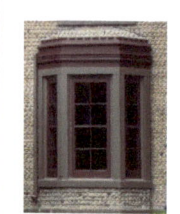
Brackets: a decorative or weight-bearing structural element which forms a right angle with one side against a wall and the other under a projecting surface such as an eave or roof. Example: 716 Watts Pond Road, Page 46	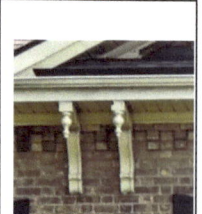
Cobblestone architecture: Refers to the use of cobblestones embedded in mortar as a method for erecting walls on houses and commercial buildings. Example: 705 Paris Plains Church Road, Page 45	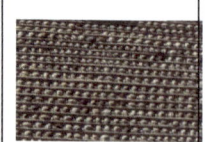
Cornice Return: decorative element on the end of a gable. Example: 705 Paris Plains Church Road, Page 45	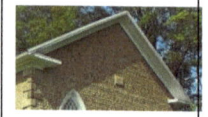
Dormer: (French for "sleep") a gable end window that pierces through the plane of a sloping roof surface to create usable space in the top floor or attic of a building by adding headroom. Example: 96 German School Road, Harrisburg, Page 34	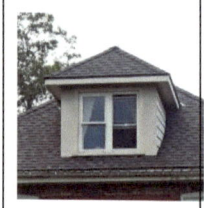

Frontispiece: a portion of the façade of a building, usually a centred doorway that is slightly raised from the rest of the building, usually with extensive ornamentation. Frontispieces are usually Classical in design with white columned porches. Example: 71 Kitchen School Road, Page 30	
Gable: the triangular portion of a wall between the edges of a sloping roof. Example: 33 Oak Avenue, Page 25	
Hipped Roof: a roof where all sides slope downwards to the walls with no gables. Example: 30 St. Andrew Street, Page 17	
Iron Cresting: A decorative ornament along the top of a roof. Iron cresting was popular in the Baroque era and also in Italianate, Victorian, Second Empire and Queen Anne styles of architecture. Example: 31 St. Andrew Street, Page 17	
Keystones and Voussoirs: a voussoir is a wedge-shaped element used in building an arch. A keystone is the central stone that locks all the stones into position, allowing the arch to bear weight. A keystone is often enlarged and embellished. Example: 31 St. Andrew Street, Page 17	

Lancet Window: a tall, narrow window with a pointed arch at its top. Example: 705 Paris Plains Church Road, Page 45	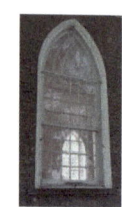
Mansard Roof: This style was popularized by Francois Mansart (1598-1666), an accomplished architect of the French Baroque period and especially fashionable during the Second French Empire (1852-1870). This roof is almost flat on the top section, with two slopes on each of its sides with the lower slope at a steeper angle than the upper and having dormer windows. Example: 87 Willow Street, Page 13	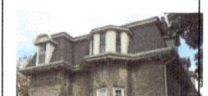
Palladian Window: a large window that is divided into three sections with the centre section larger than the two side sections and usually arched. Example: 33 Oak Avenue, Page 25	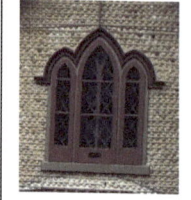
Pediment: a triangular section above the horizontal structure (entablature), typically supported by columns. The inside of the triangle is called the tympanum. Example: St. Andrew Street, Page 21	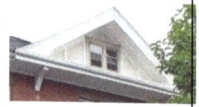

Quoin: masonry blocks at the corner of a wall, often a decorative feature, usually larger or of a different colour than the rest of the wall. Example: 705 Paris Plains Church Road, Page 45	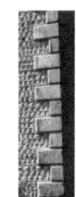
Verge boards, also called bargeboards – hang from the projecting end of a roof and are often elaborately carved and ornamented. **Finial:** ornament added to the top of a gable, pinnacle, canopy or spire – a Gothic element. Example: 23 Princess Street, Glen Morris, Page 40	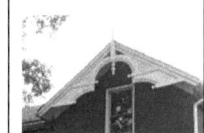

Building Styles

Edwardian, 1900-1930 – This style bridges the ornate and elaborate styles of the Victorian era and the simplified styles of the 20th century. Balanced facades, simple roof lines, dormer windows, large front porches, and smooth brick surfaces are its characteristics. Example: 111 Willow Street, Page 10	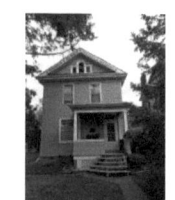
The **Farmhouse** is a country home style that highlights the simplicity of rural living. Comfort and function are the major themes that are associated with the style. The large porches were designed to help cool the interior of the home and also provide a shady spot for guests to gather and enjoy the outdoors. The architecture of a country home is minimally ornamental but very efficient with functional shutters, decorative porch railing, and dormer windows that increase interior light and living space. Farmhouse floor plans are usually square or symmetrically shaped, sometimes with side wings. The interior has a large country kitchen and a cluster of bedrooms on the upper level. Farmhouses contain at least one fireplace and large family gathering areas designed for relaxation. The country home is casual, functional and comfortable. Well-crafted and sturdy, farmhouses are generally built to last and withstand for ages. Example: Harrisburg, Page 33	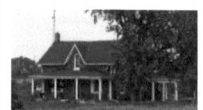

Georgian, before 1860 – This style began with the British King Georges in the 18th century. These buildings have balanced facades around a central door, medium-pitched gable roofs, and small paned windows. Example: 109 Harrisburg Road, Harrisburg, Page 32	
Gothic Revival, 1830-1890 – These decorative buildings have sharply-pitched gables with highly detailed verge boards, pointed-arch window openings, and dichromatic brickwork. It is a common style in Ontario. Example: 78 Harrisburg Road, Harrisburg, Page 31	
Italianate, 1850-1900 – It has wide-bracketed eaves, belvederes, wrap-around verandahs. Example: 15 Baird Street, Page 8	
Ontario Cottage - one or one-and-a-half story buildings with a cottage or hip roof. The cottage roof is an equal hip roof where each hip extends to a point in the center of the roof. The hip roof has a long hip in the center. The Ontario Cottage is the vernacular design of the Regency Cottage which generally has a more ornate doorway and a partial or full verandah surrounding it. The roof can have a dormer, a belvedere, and generally two chimneys. Example: 207 West River Road, Page 29	

Regency Cottage, 1830-1860 – This style originated in England in 1815 and spread to Ontario later in the 19th century as British officers retired to Canada. It is a modest one-storey house with a low-pitched hip roof and has a symmetrical front façade. Example: 899 Keg Lane Road, Page 28	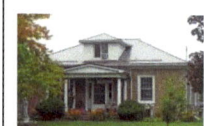
Second Empire, 1860-1880 – The mansard roof is the most noteworthy feature of this style and is evidence of the French origins. Projecting central towers and one or two-storey bays can also be present. Example: 87 Willow Street, Page 13	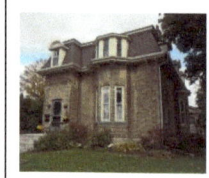

www.ingramcontent.com/pod-product-compliance
Lightning Source LLC
Chambersburg PA
CBHW040242220526
45473CB00001B/334